PETER DYNAMITE

"Twice-Born" Russian

*The story of Peter Deyneka–
missionary to the Russian world*

**Norman B. Rohrer
and
Peter Deyneka, Jr.**

D0068132

Baker Book House ● **Grand Rapids, Michigan**

ISBN: 0-8010-7639-0
Copyright 1975 by Baker Book House Company
Printed in the United States of America

Third Printing, May 1977

Contents

Foreword 7

Introduction 9

1. "Sure, All Right" 13

2. Visions of a Dying World 27

3. Five Million Corpses .43

4. Upside Down for God .51

5. A Bride for Peter Dynamite 61

6. Blazing New Trails 71

7. A Mission Is Born 83

8. One World, One Message 93

9. South to the Harvest .109

10. The School That Prayer Built 123

11. Fruit in New Orchards 135

12. No Roof over Russia .147

13. A Famine of Bread 159

14. "Much Prayer, Much Power!" 169

15. The Cry from the Steppes 183

Peter Deyneka, shown here in typical
Russian garb, has traveled to
thousands of churches in America
and around the world telling the
story of Russia's spiritual needs.

Foreword

You can't be with Peter Deyneka very long without God
doing something special for your soul. Just being with him in
casual conversation is a blessing, and listening to him preach
(in his own inimitable Russian accent and style) fills your
heart so full that you want to shout. But the greatest blessing
of all is praying with Peter Deyneka. I can never forget those
all-night prayer meetings that he conducted for us in past
Youth for Christ days. "Much prayer—much power!" was
more than a motto in those difficult days: it was the secret of
God's blessing, and it still is.

Peter Deyneka was one of the first friends to telephone me
when I came to Moody Church. "I want to come over and
pray with you," he said; and he did—and God answered.
Many times we've been on our knees in my study, crying out
to God for His blessings on our lives and ministries. What a
prayer warrior he is! What answers we have seen! God bless
Peter Deyneka for teaching so many of us how to trust God!

This book will get to your heart. None of the facts are
exaggerated or embellished; the life and ministry of
Russian-born Peter Deyneka needs no embellishment. For
over fifty-five years, God has given Brother Deyneka a
great missionary vision for lost souls—not only for the evangelization of his own Slavic people but for others as well.

Moreover, through the ministry of this dynamic revivalist, thousands of young people around the world have given their lives to Christian service.

As you read this book you will find your faith growing —your desire for prayer increasing—your concern for lost souls deepening. When this starts happening, then surrender yourself afresh to the Lord and do whatever He tells you to do. God will use you, as He has used Peter Deyneka, to touch the lives of others and help to reach a lost world for Christ.

It is a privilege to know Peter Deyneka; it is an awesome responsibility to serve as chairman of the board of the Slavic Gospel Association, which he founded. My prayer is that the reading of this book will do for you what knowing Peter Deyneka has done for so many of us. If your heart is open to the Lord, I believe it will.

Warren W. Wiersbe, Senior Minister
The Moody Church
Chicago, Illinois
1975

Introduction

Golden rays of a Siberian sunrise were illuminating the gabled peak of their sanctuary as Russian believers streamed inside to worship one morning in 1965. Many who had no Bibles of their own had braved the chill dawn to hear a pastor read from the pulpit Bible. Soon the church was jammed with over two thousand worshipers united in prayer.

"Oh, God!" cried a young man, his voice trembling. "Save millions of our people here in Russia through the gospel broadcasts!"

"*Yes, Lord, hear his prayer*," the congregation responded instantly in unison.

"Encourage our brothers and sisters who are in difficulties," a weeping grandmother prayed.

"*Yes, Lord*," came again the great, swelling response.

"Bless our brethren in other countries who are evangelizing our nation with the long arms of radio," added an elderly man.

On the high platform that Sunday morning stood a tall, balding visitor. He carried an American passport but he had the tongue of a native Russian. At the mention of the radio ministry the visiting speaker wept. Fifty years earlier he had left Russia for the New World. There he had found not only a

Peter Deyneka, preaching in Russia to a church jammed with believers, many of whom listen regularly and eagerly to Russian Gospel broadcasts.

Large crowds of believers gathered around Peter Deyneka after a morning service in a Russian church to thank him for the "bread from heaven" over the radio waves.

new world but a new life, a personal revolution through the gospel of Jesus Christ.

In his preaching to millions of people . . . in his traveling over two million miles on the King's business . . . and in his establishment of a missionary-sending agency to the Slavic world, the man had been the first to preach the gospel by radio to the vast reaches of the Soviet Union.

And now, once more among his own people, the visitor had discovered that the radio broadcasts were a most fruitful means of evangelizing a closed, atheistic land.

Half a century! Yet so great was Peter Deyneka's joy that he wished somehow he could turn back the calendar of passing years and walk with his Lord again over the same pathway of tears and triumph.

1

"Sure, All Right!"

The westbound Limited streaked past the southside tenements, dived with a roar under the city's bower of concrete, then shuddered to a halt with a hiss of billowing steam.

"*Chicago–Union Station!*"

A teenager in dark clothing nervously clutched his suitcase and gazed apprehensively at the unfamiliar surroundings. His pockets bulged with a few remaining apples, his only food since disembarking from the Russian oceanliner S.S. *Dvinsk* and boarding the Chicago-bound train at Halifax, Nova Scotia, Canada.

"Union Station!" the conductor repeated, opening the doors with a clang.

The teenager hesitated for a moment then stepped down to the platform of the strange city. That small step would be divinely ordered to lay the groundwork for the evangelization of Slavic people worldwide, although the thought was far from the teenager's mind at that moment.

As Peter walked from the train a United States Customs officer approached. "May I see your papers?" he asked.

The immigrant lad fished in his pockets and withdrew an

envelope which he handed to the man in uniform. The papers read: "Peter Deyneka. Sixteen years old. Born, Storlolemya, Province of Grodno, Russia, 1898."

The man studied Peter for a moment. "Relatives? Do you have relatives in Chicago?"

Peter handed him a second note. "Cousin Walter Markawitz, Halsted and Maxwell Streets," it said.

The customs officer called a cab and gave the driver instructions. Peter loaded his luggage into the taxi and climbed aboard for the final leg of his long journey.

The Chicago River made him homesick for the Yaseldah that flowed through Chomsk. Perhaps even at that moment his father was fishing the night waters half a world away. "The fish know Nahum Deyneka and Nahum Deyneka knows the fish," Jewish merchants in the village would say admiringly.

The old cab rattled and whined through the cobblestone streets as the immigrant leaned back and reflected on his voyage from Chomsk in the Old World.

On March 3, 1914, many of the Deyneka relatives and friends crowded into the little house to wish the traveler good fortune. The singing, interspersed with draughts of vodka, drove away the sadness in true Russian fashion.

"Hey, Pyotr!" his brother Andrei exclaimed, interrupting the party. "Look at this—from Big Misha!"

"A whole bottle of vodka? Misha must be drunk."

"Misha says you drink to him for good luck and plenty money in America," the younger brother commanded. "First, though, show everyone here how you speak English."

The older brother was embarrassed and protested strongly. "But Andrei, I don't know much English."

"Don't be bashful," Andrei shouted. "You speak it good. I heard you. Just like a real Americanyets."

Andrei had stepped up onto a chair and clapped his hands.

"Listen, everyone! My brother Pyotr is going to show how they talk in America."

The murmur of Slavic voices grew still as the guest of honor shrugged. "My brother is making a joke," he said meekly. "I don't know much English. . . ."

The crowd shouted and clapped. "Speech!"

"He's just bashful," Andrei insisted. "Go ahead, Pyotr. Say something in English."

With a red face the young man bound for the land of opportunity mounted the chair and cleared his throat. "Sure, all right," he said quietly.

The villagers shouted and applauded. "You see?" Andrei exclaimed. "Just like a real American. Do it again, Pyotr."

"Sure. All right."

The crowd tried to repeat it. "Shoor-r. All-r-rayt." What an outlandish language English seemed to be!

In the morning Peter's father brought the rented horse and wagon that would take the eldest son to the train station.

"Please be careful, son," his mother pleaded.

"Yes, mama," Peter replied, carrying his bags to the wagon.

"Do not trust strangers."

"No, mama."

"Save your money and send as much as you can. We have borrowed many rubles to send you to America. The interest on the money is high. We will need all you can send to pay it off."

"I know," Peter said as he kissed her one last time.

Villagers waved their good wishes as Peter and his father rolled through the dirt streets in the horse-drawn wagon carrying a few suitcases and the huge bag of garlic and salami sandwiches.

The farther they rolled on the twenty-five-mile journey to the train station the more Peter's father regretted his decision to send his eldest son to America. It seemed to him as a

15

bad dream. But the one-way ticket had been purchased. There was no opportunity now to turn back.

As the train approached, the father clung to his son. "Pyotr," he sobbed, "this train will take you away from me and I may never see you again."

On March 11, Peter sailed from Libau, Russia, bound for Halifax, Nova Scotia, on the S.S. *Dvinsk*, a Russian liner. For fourteen days and nights the sturdy Russian ship tossed and churned through the stormy Atlantic.

Peter had never sailed before. Consequently, his mother prepared a lunch for him, packed to last the whole voyage. It was so large that an older friend carried it on board ship for him.

Peter went regularly to the deck for exercise and daily ate his black bread and garlic—a diet he credited with preventing the terrible seasickness that gripped so many of the other passengers.

During the first days at sea Peter had met some of the Russian sailors on the ship. The sailors conspired to trick the naive boy from the country.

"If you help us work in the kitchen we will give you meals in return," the wily sailors promised Peter.

Dutifully Peter worked for his meals all across the Atlantic. Every day he longingly looked through the window of the door leading into the ship's dining room and envied all of the "wealthy people" who were able to eat in the luxurious surroundings. It wasn't until the last day of the voyage that Peter learned that the purchase of a boat ticket also included three meals a day in the ship's dining room.

But Peter's misfortune was later to provide an excellent sermon illustration which he often used in his later evangelistic ministry. "I was like many people who are trying to work for their salvation and do not know that our heavenly Father has already provided free salvation through Jesus Christ," Peter remarked.

"Halsted and Maxwell," the Chicago taxi driver announced, motioning toward a small house as he brought his car to a stop.

"Poyditye vi," Peter spoke excitedly in Russian to the driver.

The cabbie understood and went to the door. "There's a young man here from the old country," he announced to the boarder who appeared at the door.

"Is anyone expecting you?" the man asked.

"Sure, all right," Peter replied.

When Walter Markawitz returned from work at six he was surprised to find young Peter there. "My house is already full of boarders," Walter sighed, "but you might as well stay."

Peter cried himself to sleep that night in the strange city. If only his elder brother Stephan had lived. He was the one who had been chosen to seek the family's fortune in America.

What if I fail! he thought. *What if mama and papa, Vasili, Maksim, Andrei, Ivan, Anastasia, and Tekla lose the house and the land they mortgaged to send me to America!*

One hundred dollars—that was the equivalent of two hundred rubles. If he could earn that much, the Deynekas could pay all their debts and be relatively wealthy.

Peter listened in the darkness to the hum of the city. The new country was alive with industry and progress. The Markawitzes' house was warm. Perhaps he would not have to take his turn sleeping on top of a brick oven as he often did in Russia when winter came.

War clouds drifting even then toward Europe were little heeded in the New World prosperity of 1914. The lonely boy could scarely imagine that the unseen hand of Providence had brought him halfway around the globe like a chess maneuver in a strategy for evangelical outreach that one day would bless millions of Russian people. This frightened

17

Peter's humble, thatch-roofed home in the village of Chomsk in White Russia.

The sad, long ride by horse-drawn wagon to the train station and far-distant America.

First photograph of Peter, a determined sixteen-year-old, upon his arrival in Chicago, a photo which he promptly sent to his parents in Russia.

A happy Peter Deyneka with the smile that "wouldn't go away," after his conversion on January 18, 1920.

Peter with evangelist Paul Rader, his pastor, mentor, and friend—the man who challenged him to step out by faith.

young immigrant with no money, no job, and no living faith seemed at that moment an unlikely candidate for such a historic career.

Peter's first sunrise in the new world found him on the street, joining the unemployed who were seeking work. Gradually the refrain became familiar: "That's all we're hiring. No more today!"

Peter would bow and reply, "Sure, all right," and go home disappointed. But he would try again, for he had adopted the motto of his new city: "I will!"

Chicago was rapidly becoming America's second-largest metropolis. In this growing city it was appropriate that young Peter should find his first job in a lumberyard supplying building material. He earned $6.90 a week. No assignment was too hard for his eager hands, except when he didn't understand the orders.

One day the foreman gave Peter hurried instructions.

"Sure, all right," Peter replied, afraid to admit that he had understood nothing.

When the foreman returned to find the job undone he threatened to fire the Russian.

"Sure, all right," Peter replied, looking around for "fire." But he wasn't fired, and left the following year for a better job at the Crane Company's machine shop. Crane paid its employees in refined gold, handing out little envelopes with the precious ore as paychecks.

Russian immigrants in Chicago who were activists with the International Workers of the World began calling on Peter. Twice a week they would visit him at the Markawitz home, urging him to join their ranks.

"We're going to change the world!" they boasted. "There is no God. We're going to make the world better ourselves!"

Peter hesitated. His ties to the Russian Orthodox Church were strong. "There are two gods," his mother had told him. "One is in heaven, the other is the Czar of Russia." But the constant outpouring of propaganda by the Chicago atheists finally convinced him they were right.

22

Half a world away, the Deyneka family lived in daily suspense. If Pyotr failed in the New World, all their hopes of freedom from servitude to their lenders would be gone. He told them nothing of his new allegiance to atheism, nor that he attended meetings of the I.W.W. He sent his family as much money as he could squeeze from his small paycheck, living on dried bread and salami, and spending an occasional dollar for theaters, dancing, smoking, or drinking. Still there was an emptiness in his heart and he was searching in vain for lasting peace. However, his hard work and thrift paid off the family debt in one year.

On a Sunday afternoon stroll, Peter suddenly heard the strains of a hymn in his native tongue from five Russian men at Union and Thirteenth streets. He listened warily from a safe position across the street. That afternoon in 1916, as a lad of eighteen years, he heard for the first time the revolutionary message that Christ died for sinners, and that by faith in Him a believer could have peace with God. The meeting finally broke up and Peter went home.

The following Sunday he was back, this time gathering courage to cross the street and talk to the Russians.

"If you receive the Lord Jesus Christ, He will save you from sin," the strangers promised. "You would not need to drink or go to dances to find joy."

Peter shook his head. Surely these were the only five men in the world who believed such a message.

The weeks passed. Peter moved to a home where he lived with several Russian-Americans. He studied newspapers to learn English and to enjoy the pictures.

"Look here," he exclaimed one evening as he settled down to read. "A baseball player is preaching on the east side."

"That's Billy Sunday," his roommate replied as he dressed to go out.

"I want to hear him," Peter announced.

"If you go, don't take any money."

"Why not?"

"They might rob you."

Peter looked at the article again. He decided to see the ball player regardless of the "danger." Just in case his roommate was right, he took along only a dollar.

He found the hall packed with people. They made the walls ring with their singing. Homer Rodeheaver played an instrument which Peter later learned was a trombone. In Russia, the Orthodox priest was a symbol of fear; but in America, Peter noticed that the people seemed to be happy in their churches.

Billy Sunday paced the platform as he began to preach. Peter winced when he smashed a chair to illustrate a point in his lightning delivery. Peter gripped the dollar bill in his right pocket and wondered when the "robbery" would take place.

He didn't understand the invitation to receive Christ. When he spotted a personal worker looking at him he gripped his dollar more tightly. When the man walked up and extended his hand Peter held on to his money and extended his left hand. As soon as he could, he escaped into the streets, vowing he would never go to such a place again.

"What did Sunday have to say?" his roommate asked.

"He talked about Jesus Christ."

"Is that all?"

"That's all I could understand," Peter admitted.

A Russian couple, with intentions like Priscilla and Aquila of the New Testament, invited young Peter to live in their house. They saw the move as an evangelistic opportunity; Peter viewed it as a chance to eat homemade borscht and speak Russian again.

"Don't worry," he promised his buddies. "I'll never believe that Christian stuff."

Often when believers came to the home Peter would flee to his room and shut the door. He heard that the entire local evangelical Russian church was praying for him, but he resolutely held to his pretended atheism. He remained in that home for only a few months, finally moving in exasperation to an American home. He remembered that the Christians he had heard on the street corner told him he could hear eloquent English spoken by a "public speaker" in a place called "Moody Memorial Church" on Clark Street and North Avenue.

He expected to find a small auditorium with a handful of old people. Instead he found four thousand people of all ages sitting on wooden benches in a huge tabernacle with sawdust sprinkled on the floor.

"More Christians!" Peter murmured. He was tempted to leave, but the beauty of the music held him. Besides, it was Sunday and there was nothing better to do.

As Paul Rader amplified his sermon, Peter felt smaller and smaller. He was convinced that someone had tipped off the preacher about the young Russian's sinful life.

"You, there, you need to be born again!" Rader shouted time after time, pointing his long finger at the audience, always seeming to pick Peter out of the crowd. His heart raced. How could this man know so much about him—a total stranger?

Peter detected another voice that evening, a conviction inside him, speaking unmistakably: *You are a lost sinner . . . Christ died for you . . . whosoever believes in Him will not perish.*

But the counselors frightened him, so Peter left to return another Sunday for the "free English lessons" and the soul-inspiring music. He obtained a "Jesus Saves" button for his lapel so personal workers wouldn't bother him and ask to take him to the prayer room. He was suspicious about what went on behind the closed doors up front.

One Sunday Peter attended the young men's Bible class taught by the Reverend Harry Herring at three o'clock Sunday afternoons. Seventy-five young men attended this lively Bible class. At the close of his Bible message, Mr. Herring asked, "Would you raise your hand if you would like to be remembered in prayer today?" Peter raised his hand.

That Sunday night Peter wore his "Jesus Saves" lapel button to the evening service. After a great evangelistic message, Paul Rader invited those who wanted to accept the Lord as their personal Savior to come to the altar. During the invitation Peter whispered to a friend who sat near him, "You ought to go forward and get saved."

"I'll go if you'll go with me," came the reply.

"Okay. Let's go."

Peter outwalked his friend and bravely went first into the prayer room where Christian workers with their Bibles were ready to help those seeking salvation. Peter knelt and wept before God, realizing he was a needy, lost sinner without Christ.

That night Peter left the old life behind. His days forever after would be different. The date was January 18, 1920. Peter was twenty-two.

His landlord noticed Peter's broad smile when he returned home that night. "What's wrong with you, Peter? Are you drunk?" he asked.

"No, I'm not drunk. I'm saved."

"Go to bed. You'll feel all right in the morning." However, Peter couldn't sleep all that night from joy.

The smile arose with him the next day. "Peter," his landlord objected, "You're still drunk."

"No," Peter insisted, "I'm a new person."

God had "sought for a man among them, that should make up the hedge, and stand in the gap before [Him] for the land." And He had found him.

2

Visions of a Dying World

Centuries ago the Russian Orthodox monk, Philotheus, in a burst of patriotism and piety, exclaimed, "Light and truth have found their eternal home in Moscow!"

Peter Deyneka had found the light and truth not in Russia but in the New World. He came to America restive and withdrawn. Now he could not talk to enough people to share the joy of his spiritual birth. He found himself testifying for the Lord at work, on street corners, in gospel missions, and to individuals wherever he met them. Each conversation fired his zeal hotter, causing him to grow in his determination to become a soul-winner.

He joined Moody Memorial Church and attended all the meetings. He was present at Bible conferences, became elected president of the large young men's Bible class at Moody, joined the Ushers' Band to expand opportunities to speak to people about Jesus Christ, and somehow found time to enroll for evening classes at Moody Bible Institute.

In testimony meetings Peter was always first on his feet. Pastor Paul Rader at Moody Church noticed the young firebrand who became known to the congregation fondly as "Peter Dynamite," a play on his last name.

Peter seldom attended church without soldiers, sailors, policemen, or children in tow.

On July 25, 1921, Peter was baptized at Cedar Lake, Indiana, where Moody Church sponsored Bible conferences. While working at the camp, Peter looked for young men to talk to about Christ. One Sunday afternoon near the railroad station, where many vacationers were waiting for the train, he gave his testimony at a street meeting. Peter noticed two young men sitting nearby on a bench, dressed for an evening out. Peter approached them and asked, "Do you mind if I sit between you?"

They studied him for a moment then moved over to give him room. "We're going to the dance," they said.

"You should come to the gospel meeting tonight."

"No, we have dates with two girls at the dance hall," they replied.

"Well, I'm going to pray for you tonight that the Lord will save your souls. You come to the conference grounds at any time and ask for me."

The young men laughed and quickly left.

Back at the conference grounds Peter found a Christian brother and asked him to pray for the two men heading for the dance. Two hours later the same two men came to the Bible conference grounds and asked for Peter Deyneka. "Do you remember us?" they asked.

Peter nodded. "Glad to see you again," he said.

"We came to tell you that we want to accept the Lord Jesus Christ as our Savior. Will you pray for us?"

Peter quickly took them to the prayer room behind the tabernacle where they were wonderfully converted.

"Why did you leave the dance?" Peter asked.

They explained that after he talked to them at the station they were uncomfortable. While they were dancing, some misunderstanding arose between them and their girl friends.

Disgruntled, they left their dates to see Peter. Those men were two of many people the young Russian led to Christ during his frequent trips to Cedar Lake.

Each Sunday afternoon Peter's Bible class met at Moody Church from 3:00 to 4:00 P.M. After the class, Peter would cross North Avenue and hand out tracts in Lincoln Park as he spoke to strangers about the Lord. The park was usually sprinkled with sailors in training at the nearby Great Lakes Naval Training Station on the northern edge of Chicago.

One day Peter noticed two sailors on a bench in the park. He also spotted three sailors on another bench. First he approached the two and asked, "Are you looking for real joy?"

"Of course!" they replied sheepishly.

"Well," Peter explained, "let me tell you how you can find the greatest joy in the world."

For several minutes he boldly shared his testimony with them. "If you would like to know more about how to get this joy, come and hear a great preacher at Moody Memorial Church tonight," he said, pointing to the nearby wooden tabernacle that was then Moody Church. "Meet me at 6:30 and we'll have something to eat first."

The agreement was made, so Peter made his way to the three sailors on another bench to repeat the invitation.

At 6:30 he bought hot dogs for five sailors and then took them to the service, seating them in the front row. A brass band played vigorous music for half an hour while the people gathered. A choir of two hundred sat behind the speaker. The music set the spirit for the message by Paul Rader. At the invitation, all five sailors looked at Peter for encouragement, wondering what to do. Peter nodded. "Sure, go ahead, raise your hands," he whispered. All five obeyed.

The congregation began singing, "Just As I Am," and people moved forward to the counseling rooms. Again the sailors looked at Peter. He nodded. One of them whispered, "If you don't mind, we'd like you to come with us."

29

"Sure, I'll be happy to," he said, getting up and starting for a prayer room with his five charges in tow. Since he had told them all he knew in his broken English, he waited outside while the counselors spoke to the men about their eternal salvation. He knew when they came out of the room that each had taken the step of faith. Their faces shone. They hugged Peter and thanked him for introducing them to Jesus Christ.

"Now we go for lunch again," he said. This time they enjoyed something more substantial.

The five sailors scattered to the four winds, but for a long time they kept in touch through correspondence.

In the early days of his Christian life, Peter attended all the missionary conferences planned by Moody Memorial Church. In one service Peter was unusually attentive because Pastor Rader continually made reference to the need for workers in the "corn" field. Was it actually so? Did the Lord need workers in the "corn" field?

Peter listened hard. He wanted to hear of a need for workers among his own Slavic people, but the speaker did not mention Russia. He called for workers in the "corn" field instead.

At the close of the meeting Peter responded to the invitation. His heart was so moved that he wanted eagerly to serve the Lord wherever the need was greatest, even if it meant the corn field. Only after the service had ended did he discover that Pastor Rader was appealing for workers in the "foreign" field!

Many Christians since have understood clearly the need for workers in foreign fields and have done nothing. Peter misunderstood the call and was hazy on the conditions. But he obeyed first and learned the conditions later.

A far-seeing member of Moody Church named Andrew Wyzenbeek operated a thriving machine shop in Chicago. This Christian businessman's policy was to hire a certain number of young men who might be inexperienced but who

30

needed a job as they prepared themselves for Christian service.

Mr. Wyzenbeek held daily prayer meetings and Bible studies for employees in his machine shop, and encouraged his young men to actively pursue their commitment to the Lord's work.

Peter Deyneka became one of Mr. Wyzenbeek's protégés. Every day the employer spoke to Peter about pursuing his Christian training. This big-hearted, generous man paid Peter well, and was a valued friend in setting him on the path of full commitment.

After working for several seasons in Wyzenbeek's machine shop, Peter felt ready to take the step toward Christian training. He sought advice from Pastor Rader. In the church office, while they discussed his plans, Mr. Rader reached for the telephone and called St. Paul, Minnesota. President J. D. Williams of St. Paul Bible School, he explained, could arrange Peter's enrollment in that school for the 1922 fall term. Right there on the phone the enrollment was completed. Peter was on his way to school.

That summer Peter worked at Cedar Lake Christian Conference Center with his boss, Andrew Wyzenbeek. One of their fellow street-corner evangelists was V. Raymond Edman. When Peter left for St. Paul that autumn, Edman went to Nyack Bible Training School. Edman was affiliated with the Christian and Missionary Alliance and eventually became president of Wheaton College in Wheaton, Illinois. Many years later Peter Deyneka, Jr. was enrolled in that institution, and received his college training in the school directed by his father's former colleague.

Young friends at Moody Church obeyed their pastor's advice to "fill Peter's pockets with money" at a surprise send-off party, providing the means of travel to Bible school.

In St. Paul, Peter enjoyed a series of life-changing experiences. President and Mrs. J. D. Williams took seriously their responsibilities in guiding the school. They spent many hours in prayer for the student body and the progress of the institution. Many times they would take a hotel room in St. Paul and spend the entire day in prayer concerning the needs of the school and its students. Thus all the activities were bathed in intercession. The new student noted this and never forgot the lessons on the power of prayer.

The school was located in a renovated old mansion in the "Midway area" between St. Paul and Minneapolis. Peter's first professor, Harold Freleigh, was impressed by his new student's zeal and helped him through discouraging times. Often the Russian lad was ready to quit academe because he couldn't master English grammar. Mr. Freleigh would call together a few students who were Peter's special friends and who knew how to talk to the Lord. Together they would "pull Peter Dynamite through."

School policy directed that each Friday afternoon students would engage in personal work, distributing tracts and talking to people. Saturday nights found them at a downtown mission, leading the meeting. These assignments appealed greatly to Peter. During his first year he personally led sixty-five people to Christ.

One of his trophies was a Frenchman whom Peter met on University Avenue at the Midway in St. Paul. The stranger approached Peter with a piece of paper asking in a heavy accent, "Do you know where I can find this address?"

"No," Peter admitted, "but I can show you the way to heaven."

The Frenchman looked at him curiously. "The way to heaven?"

Peter nodded.

"Before you tell me the way to heaven I would like to find my way to this factory," the Frenchman insisted.

Peter quoted John 14:6 and talked to him for approximately twenty minutes. Finally the Frenchman put the note in his pocket. "Please show me, for I want to know the way to heaven," he pleaded.

A Russian and a Frenchman, standing on a street corner in America, talking about the heavenly kingdom and how they might meet there later on. Peter took the man to the Alliance Tabernacle a few blocks away. The door was locked, so they climbed in through a window—Peter first, the Frenchman following. Inside they knelt and prayed for salvation as the Frenchman poured out his heart to Christ and asked for the free gift of salvation. He later went back to France as a Christian missionary.

Peter's zeal was boundless. He started a men's all-night prayer meeting at the school, to which an impressive list of missionaries and Christian leaders trace their spiritual maturing. Many times small brush-fire revivals would spring up in those prayer meetings as students were reconciled to each other and became more earnest in their zeal for God. These Friday night prayer meetings continued for many years after Peter graduated.

One of the students had been annoyed by Peter's loud prayers. A contentious spirit arose in his heart. At 3:00 A.M. during an all-night prayer meeting one Friday, he said, "Peter, I'd like you to go down to the trunk room with me."

"Why go to the trunk room?" Peter asked. "If you have something to tell me, do it right here."

The man exclaimed, "I want you to forgive me. I have been your enemy for two years. I have criticized you and carried a grudge, and it's made me miserable. Now God has broken my heart and I want to make it right with Him and with you."

Others in the room had stopped praying and were listening. They all began praising God for this victory. The meeting lasted until 7:00 in the morning, when they all had breakfast together. Usually the all-night meetings would start with a full room, ending up with approximately a dozen.

The Lord sustained Peter Deyneka physically, spiritually, and mentally during his years at St. Paul. Down on his knees scrubbing dormitory floors in those cold Minnesota winters, Peter learned obedience. As he scrubbed he prayed, and he was able to remain in school with all bills paid at the end of the term in the spring of 1925.

For the graduation exercises of his class he was chosen to give the address. His English was the poorest in the school but his heart was the hottest for the eternal things that mattered most.

The energetic Russian student won lasting friendships among the students at St. Paul. In his autograph book they wrote their endearments. Among them are the following excerpts:

> Remember as you journey along the straight and narrow way that you have a friend that will *never, never* forget you. God has many, many people in this old world but only one like you, Pete. I love you because God made you just like you are.
> —Ernie Brown
> Omaha, Nebraska

> I thank God for the day I met you and for leading me to accept Christ as my Savior. [I] will always remember the good times we have had in room 14. Thank you for all your advice and your prayers. . . .
> —Roy Petersen
> Dawson, Minnesota

> I love you because the love of Christ dwells in you. I shall never forget the blessed times we had together in prayer and in fellowship these days at the Alliance Bible School. Though we will soon be separated one from another, we still will meet at the blood-bought mercy seat. I trust the Lord will keep you humble at the feet of Jesus and continue to use you to pluck the brands from the burning. . . .
> —Oliver K. Cedar
> Bethel, Minnesota

Always be yourself with Christ added.
—Leona Kjorth
St. Paul, Minnesota

Your ringing testimonies for our loving Lord I shall never forget. They have meant much to me. I praise God that you are one of the happy family that have greatly influenced my life. I am so thankful that I ever knew Peter the Russian, a child of the King.
—Cora Belle Nuing
St. Paul, Minnesota

Following his first year at St. Paul, Peter returned to Chicago and became a night watchman at the Chicago Gospel Tabernacle where Paul Rader was now involved in an evangelistic outreach. The "Tab" had meetings every night, but the sides of the building were open and its two grand pianos on the platform had to be guarded. At night policemen would often come into the tabernacle to relax or to warm themselves. Peter led many of them to Christ.

In 1924 Peter was assigned by the president of St. Paul Bible School to help start a new gospel church among European immigrants and others in Aberdeen, South Dakota. The new congregation also conducted meetings in schoolhouses throughout the area and Peter found himself spending the entire summer in this type of pioneer ministry.

The United States government was giving these immigrants free land if they would homestead in North and South Dakota. They started coming in droves in the early part of 1900 and many thousands of Russians eventually came to these states to farm. In fact, there were large Russian settlements there. One of the towns in this area was called Kiev and so, at the advice of Mr. and Mrs. Steven Tovstenko, Peter was encouraged to go to Butte, near the United States city of Kiev some five hundred miles west of Minneapolis.

Peter often participated in those early days at the great evangelistic campaigns and Bible conferences at the Cedar Lake Conference Grounds in Indiana.

When Peter dedicated his life for missionary service at Moody Church on June 20, 1920, he was willing to go even to the "corn field." The young fire-brand for Christ was baptized in Cedar Lake.

Student days at the St. Paul Bible Institute with Rev. J.D. Williams and friends.

Peter loved soul-winning and joined a summer evangelistic team during his student days.

Early evangelistic efforts in tent meetings taught Peter to step out in faith and prayer.

The "Russian Cossack" evangelist rode farm horses without a saddle, inviting the farmers to his meetings in North Dakota.

In Butte, his first series of meetings was at a little school-house about eleven miles south of town. For one full week he preached. The place was packed with Russian immigrants as well as English-speaking people who lived in the area. The offering for the week was five dollars. Peter was quite happy with this.

It rained almost continually during those meetings. Apparently he could not use the Model T cars which members of the congregation were driving. Peter was given a horse to travel approximately four miles one way from the house where he was staying. He was so sore after he climbed off the horse that he could hardly walk into the meeting. He did this every day for a week and became a pretty sore preacher.

After the week of meetings in the schoolhouse, Peter went into Butte where he found a large Russian settlement. He obtained permission to use the facilities of an English-speaking church and tried to round up the Russian people. They were suspicious of him, even afraid. However, the people eventually got to know and trust the visitor.

In Butte he began eating Russian food again which he hadn't had at the Bible school. Mrs. Tovstenko's mother would make borscht and Peter relished all he could get. He needed nothing else.

"You can eat everything else," Peter told the people of other nationalities who sometimes gathered at the table. "I'll take the borscht."

After graduating from St. Paul, the young Russian felt the burden for evangelizing his own people increasing. The Tovstenkos, who had been working together with him in the Minneapolis area, urged him to remain in America. "Why don't you stay here?" they reasoned. "We need you to work in the United States."

But Peter said, "No, I must go back to Russia because the many unsaved there must hear the gospel," he insisted. "I must reach my own family with the gospel also."

In the summer of 1925 he made another trip westward, this

time to Webster, South Dakota, with two other St. Paul students. The team rented a hall on Main Street for three weeks and paid one week's rent in advance. They also rented chairs and installed electric lights and placed signs outside the hall to announce the meetings, not knowing one person in town.

Only a few curious children came the first night to hear the singing. But when the preaching began they ran outside.

The three evangelists—Fred Shelander, Howard Kellec, and Peter—set up sleeping accommodations on the floor in back of the hall that night, having no money left for food or lodging. They prayed until about 3:00 A.M., then spread their newspapers out and tried to sleep.

"Let's get out of here," one of the men finally suggested, getting to his feet. "I don't think it's the Lord's will for us to be sleeping on the floor."

Peter urged him to be patient, to trust the Lord and "go through." He was convinced they were being tested for a reason. "Testings and trials are good for a person," he reminded them. "They refine the soul and produce a vessel unto honor that God can use."

Shortly afterwards, a lady who had come to one of the services asked the three young men where they were staying. They told her they were sleeping on newspapers on the floor in back of the auditorium. She seemed surprised and quickly arranged for the men to stay in homes of Christians in the area.

The campaign went on, and children's meetings in the afternoon were added. As a result of those meetings a congregation was organized in Webster.

During the third night of the series, the men conducted a street meeting in front of the hall before the evening service. Howard Kellec was giving his testimony, quoting the passage of Scripture where Jesus said He would gather the chicks under His wings, even as a hen does her chicks, but they would not accept the invitation. As Howard thought of

40

the lost souls in Webster he began to weep. The South Dakotans were impressed by his genuine concern and many new people came to the service.

On another night, Howard began to sing right in the middle of his sermon. Peter asked him afterward what kind of preaching that was where you started singing in the middle of talking. But this technique became a popular addition to Peter's own preaching later on, adding great blessing in the midst of sermons, all-night prayer meetings, and revival meetings.

In Aberdeen, South Dakota, Peter later found himself in a new series of meetings. His host was a farmer who gave him a horse to ride so he could call on surrounding farmers and announce his meetings being held in a local schoolhouse.

Peter urged his plodding steed to go faster, and later complained to the farmer that he was unable to get far on the slow horse. So the next day, the farmer offered to give Peter a faster horse "if you aren't afraid to ride him." The preacher assured his host that he was not, and mounted the younger, faster animal.

"Never let go of the reins," the farmer called as he watched the horse bolt for the open road.

Once beyond the farmyard the horse went so fast Peter hardly had a chance to catch his breath. He kept going faster despite the repeated demands to stop. "Whoa! Whoa! Whoa!" Peter gasped.

Cattle and chickens scattered as the horse thundered down the road. "Lord, stop this horse!" Peter prayed.

He finally succeeded in steering the animal toward a farm but it reared on its hind legs when it got there and would not stop completely. The farmers ran out to see what was happening, in time to hear Peter shout, "Come and hear the Russian evangelist tonight in the schoolhouse!"

"I visited many farms in a few hours and well deserved the title of a Russian Cossack which I earned that day," he recalled.

The experiences on the Dakota plains seemed to toughen his resolve to continue his preaching. The following year he took a full load at school, traveled by train to Mason City, Iowa, each Friday afternoon, visited all day on Saturday, preached on Sunday, and caught an all-night train to St. Paul to arrive in time for classes Monday morning. He kept up this schedule for an entire school year until graduation the following spring.

3

Five Million Corpses

From 1918 to 1922 Peter Deyneka received no letters from his family in Russia. During that period, a famine of enormous proportions had settled on Russia, eating at the foundations of society, and halting briefly the onrush of the Bolsheviks to construct their new brand of government.

The end of the long civil war had promised to usher in a new social order. However, the devastated country could not struggle to its feet to accept the challenges. Indescribable human suffering descended upon Russia. Their society was in disarray. On top of that, a lack of rain had paralyzed agriculture, just as war had paralyzed industry.

The peasants hated the new regime's collectivism and would not agree to the prescribed ratio of earnings from their own crops. This led to a severe decline in food production that gradually threatened the cities with starvation. Transportation facilities also came to a standstill. The country was united only in a common misery in the aftermath of the terrible war. The Soviets had survived the war. Could they also survive the hazards of peace?

At the heart of the problem was the peasant. Although the

common people had theoretically gained control of the land which had formerly belonged to the rich or to the state, the peasants rapidly clashed with the government over new economic policies and responded by harvesting only enough food for their own minimum subsistence. On top of the social turmoil came unparalleled drought in the early 1920s. The impact of the twin disasters was tragedy that shocked the world.

A large section of southeastern Russia, notably the farmland around the Lower Volga, yielded practically no crops whatever. Some fifty million people faced death by starvation. An estimated five million people died from malnutrition.

At this time the Russian writer Maxim Gorky made an indirect appeal to the American people through Herbert Hoover. Many Soviets were wary of Hoover's aid, fearing he would use it as a political weapon. But on August 20, 1921, an agreement was finally reached between the American Relief Administration (ARA) and the Soviet government. By the end of September, shipments of food began to arrive in Russia.

The noble efforts of the ARA and the Red Cross could reach only a fifth of the suffering people, however. The aid continued for two years. In July 1923, grateful Russians thanked the U.S. organization and its Secretary of Commerce, Herbert Hoover. A scroll to the ARA stated that the Russian people promised "never to forget the help given by the American people through the ARA, seeing in it a pledge of the future of the two nations."

During this unprecedented calamity, the church increased its ministry to a tragically needy people.

"I cannot describe what joy we felt as we received food parcels [from the American Relief Association]," the great Russian preacher Ivan S. Prokhanov declared. "Without exaggeration I can say that the ARA saved millions of lives

44

from starvation. The Russian people who passed through those days will never forget that brotherly help from the American people.''

Hundreds of thousands of people were not as fortunate. They did not have stamina or faith enough to overcome the horror of those days. Every day the newspapers were filled with notices of suicides.

Typhus and cholera epidemics took thousands of other lives. To these the Christian believers ministered, offering prayer and reading the Scriptures.

Into the void of agony and political disarray came great opportunities for Christian witnessing through literature. The Evangelical Christian Union under Prokhanov's leadership obtained funds in America to print sixty thousand Bibles and New Testaments. These were dispatched throughout Russia to various groups and congregations. Such religious liberties were brief, and after that time importing Bibles from abroad was forbidden.

The world was watching closely in those days to see which political path Russia would follow. Would communism continue? Or would the floundering new society change course?

Peter Deyneka's family had caught the full impact of the dreadful starvation plague. Three brothers and two sisters perished from hunger before Peter learned of the tragedy.

The first letter from his family in five years arrived while he was working as a night watchman at the Chicago Gospel Tabernacle. The news was devastating. He could hardly eat or sleep, and spent entire nights in prayer for his family. His own relatives had never heard the gospel of God's grace which had revolutionized his life. His heart burned to tell his people of the hope of salvation and eternal life. Peter dispatched what money he could and prayed for an opportunity to become a missionary to his people.

During this period of tragedy he came upon a report from Oswald J. Smith who had toured Russia and its border

Peter's first missionary trip back to Russia after World War I in December of 1925. He hired a wagon to take him to his home in the village of Chomsk.

The wagon driver dressed Peter in a peasant sheep-skin coat so that his American clothes would not attract robbers.

Peter's return was saddened by the ravages of war and famine that left his native land broken and desolate.

countries on a preaching mission. The report told of spiritual awakenings in Eastern Europe and called for prayer on behalf of the people.

"How can I describe my experiences?" Smith wrote. "How can I tell what my eyes have seen and my ears heard? Words fail me as I seek to unburden my heart and convey to others the impression of my visit to the mission fields of ancient Russia. Never again can life be the same, nor my ministry continue as it was."

The report told of thronging multitudes, crowded aisles, congested pews, plaintive songs, and fervent prayers from people who had known suffering.

"Would to God I could do something to alleviate thy sufferings and point thee to the Light!" Smith wrote. "How great thy burden! How long thy night of darkness, pain, and woe!"

Peter determined in his heart that he would trust God to send him to his people with the message of the gospel. When the war was over, he cabled money directly to his parents so they could buy bread and hold on to life. This postwar cable provided the first bread his family had seen in five years.

He wrote earnestly to his family, sending tracts and long letters, quoting passages of Scripture, and urging them to accept the Lord. Many were the days when his weakened father asked to be propped up near the window where he could watch the road, hoping to see his eldest son approach.

As Peter was seeking the Lord concerning the needs in Europe, a series of evangelistic meetings in Minneapolis was offered and he took them. On August 9, 1925, while he was staying in a private home, Peter distinctly heard the call to return to Russia. He promised God he would go as soon as funds were supplied.

One morning at 6:00 A.M. a knock on the door awakened him. He found a lady with great concern on her face.

"Peter," she began, "the Lord has spoken to me about

selling my diamond ring and giving you one hundred dollars toward your trip to Russia."

Other people in the meetings also were prompted to supply funds designated for the trip, and by October 1, 1925, Peter was on board a ship bound for home. He conducted regular services on the ship, keeping on his feet as they passed through churning waters by holding on to a railing while the ship rocked back and forth.

From Bremen, where the ship docked, Peter took the train to Warsaw, Poland, taking along a trunk packed with clothing and several hundred Russian Bibles and New Testaments. From Warsaw he continued by train to White Russia (Byelorusia) and his home town of Chomsk. He hired a horse and wagon to travel the last twenty-five miles from the depot because there was no other means of transportation. The driver was afraid Peter's American clothing would invite a robber, so he threw an old sheep skin over him.

"This will make you look more like us," he explained.

They made their way safely through the woods to the little town of Chomsk, two miles from the small village where Peter grew up and which he had left eleven years earlier.

What would he find at home? Would his ailing father still be alive?

4

Upside Down for God

Shattered buildings and trees stripped of foliage for food stood as mute evidence that war and famine had stalked the land of Peter's birth since his departure for America. As part of the war settlement, the Russian border was moved, giving Poland a strip of land including Peter's hometown. (After World War II Chomsk was taken by Russia again.)

Peter arrived in Chomsk on the day of the annual market which brought hundreds of visitors to the city of three thousand people—Russians and Jews and Poles from many parts of White Russia. People from Peter's village just outside Chomsk recognized him immediately as the wagon pulled up.

"Wait here!" they cried excitedly. "We will get your mother and brother."

Peter sat on top of his trunk in the wagon and waited, fearing his treasure might be stolen if he left it. Word spread quickly that an "American" had come. Crowds of people in the market pressed close to the wagon to see the visitor and his fancy clothes and sturdy trunk.

On his high perch Peter spotted his mother rushing

51

through the crowd with a cluster of villagers in tow. She was crying. The tall son leaped from the wagon and took her in his arms.

"Pyotr!" she could only sob. "Oh, Pyotr . . ."

"Mama," he said tenderly. "It's good to see you."

"Pyotr, . . . why didn't you come sooner? Papa died only five weeks ago. He wanted to see you . . . he didn't want to die without seeing you. But now he's gone. If only. . . ."

Through her tears Anastasia Deyneka cursed the dreadful famine that had slain her entire family except Peter and Andrei. The younger brother stood silently at their side until Peter noticed him; then they embraced.

Eleven years had changed them all—especially Peter. He had written from America that he had become "a new creature in Christ Jesus." Word had spread throughout the villages that a new religion in America had "turned Peter upside down."

Peter ordered the wagon driver to carry them home. He wanted some privacy, but crowds of neighbors followed the wagon—some asking for vodka to celebrate, others asking for American money, and still others wanting to know about his new faith.

Inside the Deynekas' small, humble, thatched-roof house the three still found no peace. Villagers swarmed into the house, eager to hear Peter describe his journey to the New World. If they locked the door, people would bang on it and shake the latch until they had to open it and let them in.

"Tell me how papa died," Peter said, noticing the bed that had been arranged beside the front window.

"It was the famine which followed the soldiers," Mrs. Deyneka explained. "We had only grass and weeds. Sometimes we ground acorns, sometimes we tried to make flour from plants and rough leaves. They cut Papa's mouth and made it bleed. It was terrible." Tears tumbled down her thin cheeks.

By now the house was filled with people demanding to

hear Peter speak. Outside people were standing at the windows, pressing close to hear his tales about the faraway land. But they were disappointed.

"I have come to tell you about Jesus Christ," Peter announced. "It's true, I have become a new person. Old things are passed away, all things are new."

"We don't understand," his mother objected. "How are you a new creature? You look like my son Pyotr."

Peter found a place behind a large table and began to preach. He was the first person ever to preach the gospel of Jesus Christ in his village. Only the young people could read and write. They were eager to have Bibles.

"The first thing I am going to do is to pray and thank God for the safe journey from the United States of America to my Russian home," Peter announced.

"Look!" someone whispered as Peter prayed. "He closes his eyes! I wonder why."

Others exclaimed, "I never heard such a prayer before!"

When he had finished someone asked, "Will you please teach me that prayer too?"

Peter later announced to the disappointed villagers that as a Christian he did not drink so there would be no vodka to celebrate his homecoming. But the people stayed anyhow, hungrily taking in every word he had to say. He began speaking at approximately seven o'clock in the evening. When he finished it was nearly midnight. Still the people did not want to go away. He preached the gospel as simply as he knew how, weaving into his message information about American life and customs. Finally Andrei, who was an atheist, ordered the people to leave so the family could be alone.

"Out! Out!" he demanded angrily. "We have not had one minute alone with my brother and he just this day arrived home. Out!"

The Deynekas talked until 3:00 A.M. Exhausted, Peter lay down on a hard bench and fell asleep. But at sunrise the neighbors were pounding on the door and shaking the latch. In Chomsk, neighbors enter a house first and then greet the people they came to see. Their demands were not unusual. Rousing himself sleepily, Peter again spoke to the citizens of Chomsk of the more perfect way, of repentance and faith in the Savior of the world, whom he had come to know. No matter how long he preached, they never became weary of listening.

There were some who were not as patient. Devout Orthodox Russians objected to the evangelical message that Peter had brought to their village. They followed Peter from house to house as he led evangelistic meetings, throwing vegetables, even bricks and rocks, to show their hatred for the gospel.

"I will show you what I think of this new religion," one young man cried. He seized a hymn book and ran into the street, tearing out the pages and scattering them to the winds. "There!" he shouted. "Begone with your gospel."

Two weeks later that young man was dead of a mysterious cause. His death brought fear to the villagers. Peter's meetings were more popular than ever and hundreds of people opened their hearts to the Lord. God made the wrath of men to please Him.

Four Christian friends from a distant city arrived the second evening when they received the news of Peter's return. They had been converted in Leningrad and were eager to talk to Peter about the faith they shared. The believers sang hymns for the people, adding to the excitement of the all-day meetings.

Services were scheduled in the village where more people could come to hear Peter preach. He discovered that in other places people would often walk from five to thirty kilometers, then stand long hours until the service was over. They were not satisfied unless the meetings lasted at least three hours. Peter's heart was stirred with compassion for

The only survivors of the war and starvation in Peter's family were his mother and younger brother, Andrei.

Some of the villagers who came to see and hear Peter, the man who was "turned upside down" by religion, were converted.

New converts near Peter's birthplace, Chomsk, marching to the river for an outdoor baptismal service during the great spiritual awakening that followed.

The "Prayer House," a Gospel chapel in Chomsk built with money Peter had brought from America. A typical meeting lasted three to six hours, with most people usually standing during the whole meeting.

his people. He saw the great hunger, heard their prayers, saw their openness as they drank in the story of redemption and applied it to their own lives.

Opposition to his message came from an unexpected source—his mother and brother. Because he did not drink vodka and enjoy other worldly amusements, they were angry.

"I have no desire whatever for smoking, dancing, and drinking," he tried to explain. "Such things displease the Lord. I only long to know more of God and to live wholly for Him."

Friends and relatives insisted that Peter stop preaching. They predicted that in a couple of weeks they would have him back into the old life of sin. They pressed Peter to buy drinks for them.

For eleven months the awkwardness continued, Peter's mother and brother urging him to forget his faith and be one of them again. Often he heard coarse language as he entered the house. Cursing would sometimes continue into the night. Andrei was so ashamed of his brother that he would not even walk with him through the village. His mother abandoned her pleas and would have little to do with her eldest son.

When Peter's life was threatened and his sanity seemed to be attacked, he prayed more earnestly that God would protect him and give him rest. "Anywhere with Jesus I can go to sleep," he repeated to himself many times, remembering the refrain of an old hymn. He was beginning to understand more fully the meaning of those wonderful words. He needed God's protection at night as well as during the day.

Friends in America occasionally sent gifts of money to sustain Peter in his preaching. He used much of it to build a chapel where he could preach freely the good news of God's grace.

He bought shoes for the poor and bread for the hungry. Word traveled fast that the "rich American" was buying

Christians for his chapel. His mother was angered and embarrassed by her son's tactics. "You should know better," she scolded.

But Peter was unable to stop. One day, near the Christmas season, a poor father rushed up to him on the street and asked for something to take to his children for Christmas. Peter bought him some white bread—a delicacy as welcome as cake to that community. The father knelt right down in the mud on the street and thanked Peter.

To help the poor he purchased roasted calves for two dollars and a whole lamb for one dollar so they could be dressed and served at special church suppers.

A merchant found Peter alone one day and in a low voice asked, "How much do you pay when people join your religion?"

"Nothing!" Peter replied.

"Nothing? You are not telling me the truth, are you?" the merchant demanded.

"Yes, I am telling you the truth. I don't pay anybody to become a Christian."

"That's too bad," the merchant said, shaking his head. "I was thinking of joining your group."

Whenever anyone appeared on the street with a new pair of shoes, Peter's mother was convinced that her son had bought them with his American dollars.

"Save your money, Pyotr!" she insisted. "You will need it when you get married."

Mrs. Deyneka was unsuccessful in stopping her generous son from helping the poor. Neither could she convince him to marry the girls she had selected for him.

"Just look at all the potatoes you could have had if you had married her!" his mother complained when he turned down her first choice. Of the second girl she announced happily, "Her father will give you a cow!"

"Please, mama," Peter would object, "I don't want to marry potatoes. I don't want to marry for a cow."

He had no plans to return to America. He wanted only to continue preaching in revival meetings among his people. They wanted to know the way to heaven. Peter had found it. Why should he think of leaving?

5

A Bride for "Peter Dynamite"

Peter Deyneka went back to his native Russia a single man but he returned to America married to a quiet Russian girl from Cherniyevichi whose spiritual zeal matched his own.

Six months before their wedding day (May 23, 1926), Vera Demidovich could not have imagined that she would one day travel to fabled America as the wife of an evangelist. She had suffered much from the madness of war and the scourge of famine. While trudging over the weary three-thousand-mile trip with her family back to White Russia near Poland after World War I, her first thoughts had been how to find enough food to stay alive. She was the daughter of a schoolteacher and a part-time Russian Orthodox lay reader, but she knew nothing of the saving grace of the Lord Jesus Christ.

The Russian girl who became a valued partner in Peter Deyneka's global ministries was born in a one-room wooden house attached to a schoolhouse where her father taught arithmetic and grammar. There was a table in the room, benches around the walls, and a modern wooden floor in the Demidoviches' residence because it was part of the school-

61

Vera (Demidovich) Deyneka with Peter. Vera was the girl who walked twenty-five miles one way to hear the Gospel preached. This picture was taken shortly after the wedding on May 23, 1926.

The Deyneka wedding was an occasion for special services and evangelistic meetings. The new Gospel chapel was always overcrowded. There was no time for a honeymoon.

Many souls were won to Christ during the special meetings, and the joyful new converts were baptized in the near-by river.

Choirs such as this one accompanied the Deynekas in the special services following the wedding. Peter later told friends in America that they had plenty of "honey," but no "moon."

house. Later homes had the usual floors of Russian dirt. Her mother sang hymns and folk songs to Vera, her first baby daughter, and fed her gruel. The family spent summers on a four-acre plot of ground which yielded potatoes, lettuce, carrots, cucumbers, wheat, and some fruit. They also had cows.

Olga, a second daughter, was added as the years passed. The girls sewed pillows, embroidered tablecloths, and sang songs with their parents around the supper table.

It was customary to walk the five miles to Gorodetz with farm crops to trade what the Demidoviches had produced for household needs. Their small world was a community of relatives and friends within a fifteen-mile radius of Borisovka.

In 1914, the year Peter Deyneka left for America at the age of sixteen, Vera was eight. During the summer harvest that year, messengers announced that German army troops were advancing toward Borisovka. Vera found a small trunk and put all the precious possessions of her girlhood into it. Then she waited quietly for her father to take her away. While her sister Olga cried and complained about the ominous news, Vera sat patiently, her placid blue eyes taking in every detail.

Several days passed, then government officials rode at a gallop through the village, warning everyone that the German army would be upon them the following morning. Almost instantly the roads were jammed with refugees fleeing eastward. In addition to the scourge of war, the countryside was caught in the grip of a severe famine. Cattle were dying of thirst and crops were parched from lack of rainfall. Rivers had dried up and wells yielded the last drops to their desperate owners.

Mr. Demidovich packed as many vegetables and as much bread and salt pork as his family could carry, then led them toward the nearest railroad depot. The last train had departed, but they found a horse and wagon whose owner had abandoned them to catch the train. They appropriated the horse and wagon and traveled fifteen miles to another town, hoping and praying that another train would whisk them away from the advancing enemy soldiers.

The station was small and so was the train that stood waiting as the Demidovich family rolled up in the wagon.

"This is the last train to leave this area before the bridge is blown up," an official told them. "Get on if you can."

Railroad workers were swarming around the train, trying to find the best places to board. Some of the workers tried to keep the Demidovich family off. Many of the people had become hysterical with fear. Police managed to restore order, threatening to punish the railroad workers for keeping others off the train. "Do you think you are the only ones we're saving?" they asked.

Vera and her family squeezed into the cattle train with scant provisions—and no water. The train began to move, carrying its cargo of humanity away from the war front toward the interior of Russia. At night, fearing that the children would fall out of the train or that some weak and sickly people would be pushed out, officials nailed the train doors shut.

An epidemic of cholera swept the evacuees, taking a deadly toll among the people. The disease added a new dimension of misery to the thirsty travelers as the train rolled on. Officials spread lime on the floor of the train and on the platforms of each station they passed trying to kill the germs of cholera. Many sick people were simply unloaded and left behind to die as the train moved on relentlessly. Vera's aunt Natasha Leonovich was so miserable she wished to die, and sat among the cholera victims so she would contract the disease. But death eluded her and her misery increased.

For nearly one month the Demidovich family stayed on that train. Wounded soldiers were carried on and off as the train moved eastward. The government set up tables of food for soldiers at selected stations. Sometimes the passengers on the cattle train were also allowed to partake sparingly.

Finally the rains descended. The train would stop at little streams from which the people could drink out of dishes, saucers, and cups—whatever they could find. No one had any idea where they were going or where they would finally disembark. It was like a journey into the twilight zone of human consciousness.

The engine was a coal-burning locomotive which continually bathed the passengers with soot and heat. When coal ran out, the engineer would stop in forests where the weakened passengers would have to help cut down trees to provide fuel to keep the train going.

The depression of the passengers increased with each mile. They wept and sobbed almost continually—even men cried in those desperate days of uncertainty and suffering.

"What is going to happen to us?" they asked.

Vera's aunt Natasha recalls that there was a general feeling among the Russian people on the train that they had offended God by their sins. They considered their anguish punishment for their iniquities. But there was no one among them to point beyond the traditions of the Russian Orthodox Church to forgiveness in Jesus Christ.

Vera's mother also cried much on the journey. She was not a stoic like her husband and first daughter. Little Vera was prepared by temperament to endure the hardships better than her sister. Olga, tempestuous and lively, was given to complaining, but Vera kept to herself and said little.

A fellow teacher became acquainted with Vera's father. She invited his family to leave the train with her and settle in the city of Masalsk for the duration of the war. For one year they lived in the home of that schoolteacher—only a day's ride from Moscow. Mr. Demidovich served as a Psalm reader in the Orthodox church; Mrs. Demidovich sewed for the people in the village.

From Masalsk they eventually moved southward to the Crimea and the Caucasus near the Black Sea to remain there for two years. When the war began to wind down, their hearts turned back to White Russia three thousand miles away and they made plans to move again. It had not rained for two years in the Crimea. Famine was again a killer. But Mr. Demidovich traded some valuables for a horse so he and his family could begin the three-month journey home. They loaded their possessions on a cart and began their three-thousand-mile walk back to their home village—walking alongside their cart as the horse plodded westward, leading them to a new life of beginning again. And walking was the only way they could travel since transportation was knocked out by war and internal strife.

They had left the Crimea in the heat of summer, but it was snowing in Borisovka when they arrived. Their house had been destroyed, so they lived for a time with a grandfather and an uncle. They discovered also that the Polish-Russian border had changed so that their village was now in Poland. This meant Vera's father was no longer licensed to teach school. Russian was not the official language of Borisovka any longer. Mr. Demidovich's father had left him a bit of land, so the family settled on it and planted a new crop for a new season.

Vera helped her father work the farm. For recreation she sometimes walked forty miles to visit relatives and friends. In one of the villages she visited after one of these forty-mile treks she heard that a Russian evangelist had come to conduct gospel services. He had migrated to Canada, but out of concern for the spiritual needs of his own people he returned to Russia. Relatives took Vera along to a house meeting to hear the man and his teachings.

Some twenty people gathered in the small house that day. The Canadian immigrant and another man were the only two Christians in the entire community. As Vera listened to the message of God's redeeming love, her heart was strangely moved. Eagerly she joined the others who committed their lives to Jesus Christ. She would never be the same again.

Later her sister and mother arrived in the same village to visit relatives. Vera took them to hear the evangelists, but her family did not like what they heard. They returned home divided by the Sword of Truth. After that, Vera had to sneak out of the house very early in the morning and very quietly so she would not be hindered in her walk to the nearest Sunday services twelve miles away.

Three years later, Peter Deyneka came to that same village to preach. Vera Demidovich, the girl who "endured hardness as a good soldier of Jesus Christ," had earned a noble reputation among the congregation. Peter, too, was impressed by the twenty-year-old girl's devotion to her Lord. After they were introduced, a bond of friendship cemented their future. Both became convinced that God had brought them together to continue His work as man and wife. Six months after their meeting, Vera Demidovich and Peter Deyneka planned their wedding day: May 23, 1926.

According to the Russian Orthodox customs at that time, the couple to be married walked in a circle three times behind the priest. Other traditional customs accompanied the Orthodox ritual. But villagers who knew Vera and Peter were certain they would arrange an evangelical wedding.

On the big day, large crowds gathered early in the morning both at the little chapel in Peter's native village of Chomsk and also in the Demidovich home fifteen miles away. Peter took advantage of the occasion to preach the gospel—first at the home of his bride and later at the evangelical church in Chomsk.

A light lunch of black bread and Russian tea was served in Vera's home. From there the couple rode in separate wagons to the chapel in Chomsk for the ceremony. Many young people rode along in the wagons, singing as they bumped along on the dirt roads.

It was three o'clock in the afternoon when they finally arrived at Chomsk to greet the large crowds of waiting people. The scene reminded Peter of market day. Four policemen scurried around to keep order among the Russians, Jews, and Poles who had come to witness the wedding ceremony of evangelical Christians.

A choir in the chapel began singing "Crown Him!" followed by other songs appropriate for the occasion. A Russian Christian missionary who, like Peter, had been to America, was conveniently on hand to perform the wedding ceremony. A total of nine gospel preachers were present and they all participated in the daylong services which began out-of-doors at 8:00 A.M.

The simple dedication performed, the crowd moved en masse to the house of Peter's mother where they enjoyed a rare treat—roast veal with black bread and Russian tea. The singing continued like a benediction on the happy couple, and the sun had long since disappeared when the singing and the preaching came to an end on that momentous day.

"We had honey, but no moon!" Peter told friends in America when he described the rainy season that followed. He and Vera desired more than anything else to put the Lord's work ahead of their own ease, so they traveled on foot in pouring rain for sixteen miles to the homes of Vera's relatives to distribute gospel portions and to tell them about Jesus Christ. They arrived at eleven o'clock in the morning the following day and found that a crowd of eager people had already gathered. They would not even let the bride and groom dry their clothes. They had to begin the services immediately.

Peter preached from eleven to one o'clock, thinking that would suffice. "You're not going to go, just giving us a two-hour service!" exclaimed one mother with a six-month-old baby. "I walked twenty miles to this place to hear God's Word, and you want to quit so soon?"

There was nothing to do but have a short recess and continue another service, lasting until 5:00 P.M.

The newlyweds stayed the night with relatives. In the

morning the rain poured down again, but they set their faces toward a village twelve miles away through a woodland. They borrowed a team of horses and a horse blanket to cover their heads. Before they arrived, however, the blanket had become soaked and the dirt began to trickle down their faces. They were cold but supremely happy, doing the work of the Lord on their honeymoon.

"In the afternoon we reached the village where a crowd was waiting for us," Peter wrote. "We had a wonderful gospel service even though we were cold and tired. It was a great encouragement to witness for the Lord."

A spirit of revival followed them. Russian people eagerly responded to the message of salvation and believers were stirred in their zeal to follow the Lord more closely.

For Peter, the days of his honeymoon marked the end of a long and torturous sojourn with his unbelieving family. His family had pressured him relentlessly. Close friends urged him to return to the United States where he might find his health again and secure the support of Christian people in America for the Russian work. But since documents would have to be acquired for his wife, he would have to go ahead without her.

A tearful farewell followed in Peter's home where many skeptics gathered with the Christians. His mother and brother Andrei had not yet come to the Lord. They opposed his going, but at five o'clock the following morning he set his face once again toward the United States for the momentous events that would change the course of his life.

His first stop was the American consulate in Warsaw, Poland, where he had to prove he had enough money to care for his wife when he would bring her to the United States.

6

Blazing New Trails

As Peter sailed into New York's harbor, past the Statue of Liberty, where many of his countrymen were being processed as immigrants, his mind was fixed on the memories of his homeland. His devoted wife waited in Russia for the ticket which he must dispatch as soon as possible.

Peter thought, too, of his Russian brethren whom he had left behind on the borders of the vast country to the north. Many were willing to give themselves fully to the preaching of the gospel, but they had no funds.

Willing hearts, but no means of support, Peter mused as he stood at the rail of the oceanliner and gazed eastward. Mentally he gathered up his resources. He had nothing —nothing but the riches of Christ Jesus which were available only as willing people invested in the outreach of the gospel.

"I have seen the vision," he told Russian friends in New York City. "I have heard their cries. I cannot forget my people."

In the midsummer heat of New York, Peter began at once to seek out fellow believers among Russians to share with them his needs and his burdens. Eagerly they invited him to

71

speak of their people, to report on the revival meetings he had led across the sea.

Rev. Ivan Stepanovich Prokhanov, a Russian from Leningrad, was the principal speaker in one of those conferences. He was an engineer whose heart had been captured by the Savior and set afire for evangelism. Prokhanov was a mountain of a man with a rather high-pitched voice. He had been sent to the United States the first time by the Westinghouse Company at whose branch office he was employed in Russia. Now, as president of the All-Russian Evangelical Christian Union headquartered in Leningrad, USSR, the the missionary statesman had returned to North America to raise funds for that ministry.

Common goals and concern drew the two men to each other. On November 1, 1926, Peter Deyneka was appointed field secretary of the Evangelical Christian Union and traveling Russian evangelist in the United States and Canada for this All-Russian Union. His duties were to raise money for evangelistic work in Russia, speaking both in Russian and English churches of America.

Six weeks after her husband's appointment with the Evangelical Christian Union, Mrs. Deyneka arrived from Russia. The couple left as quickly as they could obtain passage for Chicago, the city where Peter had found the Lord, and a centrally located base selected for his ministry.

"During those early years I traveled all of the time throughout the United States and Canada," Peter recalls, "speaking at missionary Bible conventions and young people's rallies and conducting evangelistic meetings, as well as supplying the pulpits of various churches. I had the joy of seeing hundreds of people accept the Lord Jesus Christ as their Savior. And I saw many hundreds volunteer for Christian service."

As funds from the United States began flowing into Russia in the 1920s the Evangelical Christian Union gathered strength for its varied ministries. Evangelist Prokhanov

72

used his enormous influence among Christians and non-Christians alike to advance the cause of Christ in a nation that was officially atheistic.

One of the most vital needs in Russia was for Bibles, Christian literature, and hymn books. Prokhanov had earlier approached the Czarist Ministry of the Interior in St. Petersburg with a request that its printing office furnish hymn books for the evangelical churches. This department of the government had decreed in the early 1900s that evangelicals were "dangerous to church and state activities, therefore their right to assemble for services is prohibited."

Nevertheless, Prokhanov knew that its printing department was eager for business. In 1901 a governmental decree directed that no religious literature could be distributed except that which was authorized by the official government printing division—the Orthodox Church.

The planned approach by the evangelical leader caused the evangelical church apprehension. What would happen? "Don't try it!" his friends warned. "It's impossible!"

But Prokhanov would not be discouraged. He felt a bright assurance that God would make even the wrath of man to praise Him in this opportunity.

With the manuscript for the new hymnal under his arm, Prokhanov approached the director of the printing bureau of the Ministry of the Interior.

"I wish to place an order for a hymn book," he said.

The minister, an important-looking Russian, studied the title: *The Gusli* ("The Harps"). He did not know that the manuscript contained hymns used in gospel meetings of believers.

"How many copies do you want?" the director asked.

"Twenty thousand," Prokhanov stated. "And I desire to have the whole quantity printed as quickly as possible."

The printer made some notes. "All right, we will push the job," he promised. "As to the approval of the censors, you won't have to trouble yourself. We will get that."

73

Prokhanov left the department smiling. "Here I had been worried over the censors, trying for some time to cross that bridge!" he explained to friends. "And now I find the bridge was not even there!"

In ninety days the entire edition of twenty thousand copies of *The Gusli* was delivered. Believers bought them quickly, afraid that the censor from the Orthodox Church might discover the new evangelical publication and clamp his red flag on the inventory.

The Christians could scarcely believe what they now held in their hands. The edict against the publishing of any religious literature was well known. Yet there was the imprimatur of the government: "Printed in the printing establishment of the Ministry of the Interior, St. Petersburg, Fontanka No. . . ."

In America, Peter Deyneka's ministry with the Evangelical Christian Union occupied nearly all his waking hours. He had been so busy when his wife arrived from Russia that he had neglected to have a wedding picture taken.

Mr. and Mrs. Steven Tovstenko, friends of Peter in Minneapolis when he attended Bible school in nearby St. Paul, invited Peter and Vera for a visit. They arranged for a wedding picture, although the event was more than six months behind the happy couple.

Mrs. Tovstenko helped Mrs. Deyneka dress for the official photographic record of their wedding half a world away and half a year past.

The years of 1922 to 1928 marked history's fastest expansion of the gospel in Russian history. In the vanguard was the publishing of Bibles and hymnbooks. The Russian people were starved for copies of the Word of God. They bought them eagerly.

During this period of great evangelistic opportunity, the 1923 Lenin Constitution was in effect. Lenin's Constitution had allowed both religion and antireligion the right to propagandize. This meant that Christians not only had opportunity to print gospel literature, but also to preach the gospel even outside churches.

But the Lenin Constitution was changed by Stalin and most articles of the Stalin Consitution are the ones enforced today throughout the Soviet Union.

Article 124 of the Stalin Constitution reads: "In order to assure to citizens freedom of conscience, the church in the USSR is separated from the state, and the school from the church. Freedom of religious worship and freedom of anti-religious propaganda is recognized for all citizens."

In reality, Stalin's Constitution meant that while atheism can be freely propagated, religious worship is officially curtailed to registered church buildings.

During the 1920s, Prokhanov organized *The Christian* magazine. Fifteen thousand copies a month were distributed, but the evangelist impatiently called it "an insufficient supply." Such publishing enterprises were not forbidden in the Soviet Union at that time. However, the believers were hindered during those years of opportunity because of shortages of paper and money.

"It was very sad," Evangelist Prokhanov wrote. "People everywhere were asking for Bibles, but we could not supply them."

In many places, peasants offered a cow or a sack of precious grain in exchange for one Bible. Such a hunger for Bibles led to Prokhanov's return to North America. He negotiated with Christian friends who booked meetings for him in American churches. He arrived in New York on May 23, 1925, and stayed until November 1, 1926, just long enough to meet Peter Deyneka and to join forces with him. Peter Deyneka worked with Prokhanov for five years visiting churches all over the United States. Together these men raised a total of $100,000 for Russian Bibles in two years.

The first edition of the Scriptures was actually printed in Russia while Prokhanov was in America—an edition paid for by funds contributed by the American people who heard his appeals. The famine of Scriptures was too immediate to await the Russian's return home.

During the last month of 1926, the entire year of 1927, and the first five months of 1928, the Russian Christians were able to print the following:

Bibles (including those printed during Prokhanov's
    visit to North America) 35,000
New Testaments 25,000
Hymnals
    The Gospel Songs 25,000
    Spiritual Songs 25,000
    The above, with notes 10,000
Bible Concordances 15,000
The Gospel Advisor (church calendar preserved and read
    over and over throughout the year)..........40,000

Total publications: 175,000

From 1914 to 1957 this was the *only* Scripture allowed to be on the presses of the Russian government. Prokhanov calls it "a gift from God and the American Christians to the Russian people at a time of famine for the Word." The deep significance of this production and scattering of the Word of God over Russia will be better understood and appreciated if one remembers that while there was a famine of Scripture the whole of Russia was continually being flooded with atheistic propaganda.

Peter had the joy also of contributing to Prokhanov's work of training ministers at the Leningrad Bible School which the engineer-preacher founded. When Prokhanov returned to Russia from what he termed "mysterious and fascinating America," he received a multiplicity of invitations to speak.

In 1930, Prokhanov invited Peter to return to White Russia and take advantage of the partially open doors for evangelism. Daughter Ruth had been born, but both parents were

When Mrs. Deyneka at last arrived in America six months after the wedding, a reception was arranged in their honor by friends in Minneapolis.

Peter Deyneka with Ivan Stepanovich Prokhanov, a giant of a man both physically and spiritually. As field secretary of the Evangelical Christian Union, Peter was able to raise funds to help Prokhanov achieve many of his goals in Gospel literature production.

Peter Deyneka accompanied Prokhanov in revival meetings in White Russia.

After much conflict, Peter's mother was wonderfully converted and was
baptized in the river where her husband and son had fished for a living.

A new and rare experience for
Peter's mother was a ride to church
in an automobile with some American preachers.

willing for Peter to return to his people and continue his ministry.

On February 22, 1930, Peter left for his homeland aboard the S.S. *Majestic*, accompanied by a Christian businessman of Fargo, North Dakota, A. R. Scherling.

A series of side meetings led them finally to Riga, Latvia, where the two Americans found people waiting for them. They intended to close the service at noon, but the audience wept and pleaded for them to continue.

In the evening they returned for evangelistic services. Again the gospel hall was overflowing with eager listeners. The Spirit of the Lord was poured out mightily. A touch of revival inspired them, renewing their zeal to press on in the work.

From Riga they traveled through a blizzard to Tartu, Estonia, fully expecting the meeting to be canceled. But the hall was filled with Russians and Germans. Again the Holy Spirit awakened believers and brought conviction on the assembled citizens.

"We have no time for rest," Peter wrote. "They tell us we can rest at the next place. But at the next place they tell you the same thing. Now they are telling us we can rest in America!"

At each meeting in the satellite countries—Poland, Latvia, Czechoslovakia, Yugoslavia—they prayed for the suffering Christians in Russia.

When they entered White Russia, Peter grew homesick to see his mother, even though she had told him in her unbelief four years earlier never to come back home.

The men arrived by horse and wagon in the little town of Chomsk. His mother saw Peter through the window and rushed out to meet him, even before he got off the wagon.

"My dear son, Pyotr!" she exclaimed. "I gave my heart to the Lord and now I will be a different mother to you. Christ has made me a new creature too!"

Peter wept. "My prayers have been answered!" he exclaimed.

At the meeting that evening (there was always a meeting) Peter's mother stood up and told her gathered neighbors and friends, "I persecuted my son Pyotr because I was in spiritual darkness and did not know the Lord. Satan made me do many things that I did not like to do. But now, thank God, I have given myself to God. I want to live for Him."

It happened that Pastor E. Shevchuk of the Russian Evangelical Christian Church of Chicago was visiting White Russia and Poland that same week. It was he who baptized Peter's mother in the river from which her late fisherman husband had made a living. Meetings of the men in the tiny chapel often lasted for three hours. Everywhere people clamored to hear what the Bible taught.

In 1930 the evangelical church in Russia numbered nearly three million believers, according to statistics compiled by Evangelist Prokhanov.

Prokhanov reported that is was not uncommon to hear of Jewish people also being converted to Christ. He noted also that the proverbial fanaticism of Muslims was tempered, so that in some places of Russia the Mohammedans actually invited the evangelical preachers to speak about Jesus Christ in their mosques.

In 1930, opportunities for evangelism halted abruptly. Freedom to propagandize was eliminated. The Constitution of 1929 was amended to give antireligious propaganda more privileges and to deny the same to religion: no more open preaching and evangelism. But the fruitful years had swept countless thousands into the kingdom of God.

"The wonderful progress of the gospel in my country during the years of 1924 to 1930 amounted to a national gospel reformation," Peter observed. "All classes of Russian people, including the clergy—all nationalities, tribes, and occupations—were caught up in the sweeping revival. This was an answer to prayer—a miracle during a time after the Revolution when atheism officially controlled the government."

The official government magazine *The Atheist* often ran caricatures of the evangelicals. But this strategy backfired on the editors. So many readers were curious about the Christians that they sent letters asking for Christian literature to find out who they were.

"In this way," a pastor wrote, "even atheism helped us spread the gospel. It was good advertising for the moment and led to a source of new converts."

The atheists were fond of arranging so-called "antireligious debates" in the largest halls. The rooms were always filled. Usually the first speakers railed against God, religion, and moral law. Afterward the defenders of religion were allowed to speak.

It is clear from Rev. Prokhanov's records that the audiences usually interrupted the evangelical speakers and asked for the addresses of churches. As a result, new hearers filled the humble sanctuaries of the Russian believers following the well-publicized debates.

Religious bodies sometimes distrusted each other. But when the atheists came with their propaganda, all the various denominations and groups united solidly to fight back.

"The hearts of the Russian people, with their mysterious seeking after God, cannot accept the atheistic doctrine," Prokhanov wrote. "On the one hand they were disappointed in the old system of the Russian Orthodox Church. On the other hand, they had no desire to accept the new system of atheism."

Peter Deyneka did not realize that his trip to White Russia in 1930 would be the last opportunity to freely preach to the people of Russia. But there would be other ways and other workers. It was time in God's scheme for an organization that would evangelize the Russian people both in their own country and now scattering to the farthest reaches of the earth.

7

A Mission Is Born

Adverse winds in the early thirties blew shut the doors of evangelistic opportunity in the Soviet Union. Millions of citizens voted against the militant atheistic society of Russia by fleeing to other parts of the world.

In June 1931, Peter resigned as field secretary and missionary for Prokhanov's All-Russian Evangelical Christian Union and joined Pastor Paul Rader's Missionary Society based at the Chicago Gospel Tabernacle. Rader, Peter's spiritual father and mentor, had repeatedly urged the young Russian to join his staff and assist in missionary rallies. Peter seized the opportunity to burden American Christians who could help evangelize Slavic people.

On July 1, 1931, Peter became secretary of the Russian work on behalf of Rader's World-Wide Christian Couriers.

The concept for the World-Wide Christian Couriers was to establish neighborhood Bible classes by Christian people in the homes of unbelievers. The believers would bring in others and they would thus introduce them to Christ. It was purely home evangelism, and Paul Rader envisioned the concept circling the globe. Occasionally he would arrange to stage conventions, bringing together many "courier classes" in large gatherings called "Tamasha." The word was adapted from an undisclosed foreign language to describe large gatherings of people. The programs featured class manuals, coins with insignia on them, music and banners, and a variety of special speakers.

Rader launched the first Christian radio broadcast in the Chicago area. He also kept up a continual itinerary of Bible conferences and meetings to occupy the hours and days of his hard-driving ministry.

The Rader-sponsored programs gave Peter vast opportunities to expose believers to the needs of Russian Christians. Rader always put Peter in charge of prayer meetings —seasons of intercession which often lasted the entire night.

From Ivan Prokhanov, Peter had learned what God can do through a Russian with organizational abilities. Paul Rader taught Peter how to pray and how to preach powerfully with anecdotes and stories to illustrate truth and create spiritual hunger.

In September 1933, a cable summoned Peter to Slavic countries of Eastern Europe for another extensive tour sponsored by the Union of Slavic Churches of Evangelical Christians in Poland. Again the meeting halls were packed, the services long, and the spiritual hunger intense.

Late that year Peter returned from his third trip to Eastern Europe and Russia more convinced than ever that an agency was needed to call people of North America to prayer for the Slavic people to whom Peter had been divinely appointed as a missionary.

At first he fought the idea of establishing a new missionary organization. His administrative talent was untested. All he knew how to do was to call people to prayer and repentance. God would have to do the rest.

For three days, Peter and his wife prayed and fasted, trying to determine whether the divine light was green or red in the matter of establishing a mission. They paced up and down in their apartment, crying and praying—not forgetting to praise the Lord for the answer they knew would come.

Peter went to see a prominent Christian businessman to ask him to join with him in establishing a mission to Slavic people.

"Do you have capital, Brother Peter?" the man wanted to know. "Anytime you start an organization you've got to have money!"

"Well, we don't have money but we have God," Peter replied.

"Then I'll pray for you because I respect you, but I don't think I should join you," the businessman decided.

Outside, a winter rain began to fall. Peter was discouraged. To add to his discouragement he got lost on the way home in his car.

When he finally reached his apartment, his wife excitedly held up an envelope. "It's a letter from Iowa," she said.

Peter tore it open and found a check inside for $950 with a note from two elderly ladies: "Dear Friend Peter: We met you a few years ago and we remember how you told us of your desire to preach the gospel to the Russians. We are enclosing a check for $950 for your use where needed most."

Peter was so excited he immediately phoned the businessman to report the news.

"Is that all?" the voice on the other end of the line asked.

"Yes! Amen! Praise the Lord!" Peter replied.

"What do you want me to do?"

"Nothing! I just wanted to give you this report," Peter exclaimed.

That man missed an opportunity to participate in a miracle, but Peter was not without other supporters.

One afternoon while visiting with Paul Rood, pastor of Chicago's Lake View Mission Covenant Church, later to become president of the Bible Institute of Los Angeles (Biola), Peter shared with his friend his burden to organize a missionary outreach among Slavic people the world over.

Dr. Rood suggested they kneel in prayer and commit the matter to God.

As they rose from their knees, Charles Bodeen walked in to discuss a matter with his pastor. "Brother Charlie," Dr. Rood said, "Peter has a great burden to evangelize Russians. And we're going to help him."

The three men put their arms around each other and in that informal circle once again lifted their hearts to God in prayer.

The date was set for a committee meeting one week later. Five men assembled in a back room of C. B. Hedstrom's shoe store on Belmont near Clark, January 6, 1934. The Saturday afternoon weather was cold, accented by a chill wind off the lake. With Peter at that original committee meeting were Dr. Rood, C. B. Hedstrom, Dr. Arthur Brown—a medical doctor and surgeon—and George Benson, a businessman.

The name they chose was "The Russian Gospel Association," later expanded to "The Slavic Gospel Association." Dr. Rood was elected chairman of the board; George Benson became secretary-treasurer; Arthur Brown and C. B. Hedstrom were members of the Executive Committee, and Peter Deyneka was named General Director and Missionary Evangelist. The die was cast. The organization became the lengthened shadow of the "Rushing Russian" and was on its way to becoming the largest mission of its kind in the world.

"Peter Deyneka is a native Russian Christian who is on the firing line for God," Paul Rood wrote in his first letter to prospective supporters. "He has a vision and a passion for the evangelization of his people. A group of us who believe thoroughly in Brother Deyneka's sincerity and genuineness have gladly associated ourselves with him to help realize his vision.

"Christ died for the Russians as well as for all other nationalities. Multitudes among the Russians are responsive

86

to the gospel and many are being saved. The field in which our association is working is white unto harvest. Christ is coming and the time is short. What is going to be done will have to be done soon.

"We ask for your prayers."

The first gifts came from the board members themselves. Gradually the base of support was broadened to include friends that Peter Deyneka had made during the previous years of ministry.

Peter and Vera Deyneka carefully groomed their children to take part in the work to which God had called them. Not an evening passed without family prayers. When they were in high school, the children knew they could not leave the house for evening activities until after prayer. So they would sometimes hurry their parents to start the prayer time.

Ruth was given piano lessons and taught to sing and to speak the Russian language.

Young Peter was made to take Russian and piano lessons, even when he grumbled and complained. "Piano is for girls," he mumbled to his father one day, tears running down his face.

"Who's your teacher?" Peter asked.

"Mr. Merrill Dunlop," the boy reluctantly admitted.

Since Peter Deyneka had enjoyed little childhood leisure in Russian village life, he sometimes found it difficult to understand his own son's desire to play baseball and shoot marbles. Once he bent a verse of Scripture to exhort his son against playing with his collection: "Son, the Bible says, 'Marble not!'"—a unique interpretation of the inspired text.

When Ruth was only three years old, she touched her father's heart by her strong desire to be near him. The Deynekas were living in a third-story apartment in Chicago. Mrs. Deyneka had to walk down and up several flights of stairs to carry coal from the basement to heat her stove. One evening while his wife was caring for her household matters,

The first Executive Committee of the newly formed Russian Gospel Association. Left to right, seated: Dr. Paul W. Rood, Chairman; C. B. Hedstrom, Vice-chairman; Peter Deyneka, General Director. Standing: Dr. Charles Porter; Dr. Arthur I. Brown; and George A. Benson, Secretary-treasurer. A seventh member, Mr. M. D. Plunkett, was not present for the photograph.

Early picture of the Deyneka family with baby Ruth. The whole family went along to meetings if Peter was preaching in the Chicago area.

Rare moments when Peter could relax with his family were precious.

A Deyneka family portrait with all three children—Ruth, Peter, Jr., the fledgling pianist, and Lydia who accepted Christ at her father's meeting when she was five years old.

Peter was packing his suitcase to leave for a speaking engagement. But Ruthie got hold of his valise and hung on. "No, papa!" she cried. "I won't let you go! I won't let you go!"

Peter recalls the moment with tears, "I had to jerk my suitcase out of her hands; she wouldn't let me go. It nearly broke my heart. But when you say Yes to Jesus, you have to go. I could hear her a block away crying and calling out for me. I was crying too. It was not easy. My wife cried—many times. When you say Yes to Jesus, you have to pay the price."

When Lydia was only five years old, she crawled up on her father's knees one evening and said, "Daddy, when are we going for a ride? Other children go."

Peter replied, "I have no time to take you now. But on Sunday evening I'll take you with me."

The day came and it was bitter cold. "I want to go with dad!" she reminded her mother.

That evening she sat in the service and listened to her father preach. When he gave the invitation she came forward to receive Jesus Christ as her Savior. Two ladies came on his right and Lydia to his left.

"I am going to kneel down first with my daughter," Peter told the congregation.

"Lydia," he said, "do you want something from the Lord?"

"Yes, papa, I want Jesus to come into my heart and make me a Christian girl."

Peter prayed for her, then urged her to keep praying while he went to deal with the others who had responded to the invitation. To this day, Lydia points to that experience as the time when she was made a new creature in Jesus Christ.

In the summer months Peter arranged meetings so that he could take all his children along. He taught them to sing choruses and participate in the meetings.

(To Mrs. Deyneka belongs a large share of the credit for

90

raising godly children. While Peter traveled she remained at home with their youngsters. She fasted every Friday and kept the children at their lessons and their prayers, and raised their sights high toward the possibilities of Christian service. She stayed at home without traveling for more than forty years, braving a trip by airliner to Quito, Ecuador, only after her first grandchild was born.)

The mission grew steadily. When Peter ran into administrative problems he depended on the dynamism of prayer and faith. Once each month he hung a sign on the door of his office, which was in his home, announcing a day of prayer. No one was allowed to disturb the staff that day because they were giving the entire day to prayer. Those prayers watered the soil of every preaching mission.

Wherever Peter traveled, people responded to his message. Christians found the courage to surrender their talents and resources to God; the unsaved were moved to respond to God's saving grace; and people who had forgotten the needs of missions were drawn into the widening circle of staunch supporters.

As Peter traveled out from his Chicago hub he took other young people with him. Among those early team members were Walter Covich (a Chicagoan of Russian descent who taught Peter how to drive a car and who later established a work among Russians in Alaska); Const and Elizabeth Lewshenia, who became active in ministries in South America; Mary Fewchuk, who with her husband Sam served as missionaries in South America and Australia; and Andrew Semenchuk, who was later to become the director of the mission's Russian Bible School in Argentina.

The first year of the mission's outreach passed swiftly, ending on January 11, 1935, with a missionary rally in the Lake View Mission Covenant Church, Chicago.

The celebration lasted all day, beginning at 10:30 A.M. with an opening prayer by the Rev. Emil Burke, an advisory member. C. B. Hedstrom, vice-chairman of the Slavic Gospel Association, presided. Mr. and Mrs. E. Plunkett provided music. Afterward, Dr. Paul W. Rood, chairman of the association, introduced Dr. Harry A. Ironside, pastor of the Moody Memorial Church. Peter closed this session with a brief address on "Why Evangelize the Russians." The meeting closed with a session of prayer.

At 2:30 P.M. the second session opened, this time featuring a message by Dr. Bob Jones, president of Bob Jones College in Cleveland, Tennessee. "Dr. Bob" had just returned from a missionary trip to Russia.

A third session opened at 7:30 P.M., with Dr. Jones again preaching. He told how hungry the Russian people were for the gospel. He had seen many hundreds stand for nine hours one day, listening to the gospel. The message ended at 10:15 P.M.

When the crowds had gone and the offering had been counted, the executive committee and their wives knelt down in the middle of that auditorium and cried a thankful prayer to God for a most wonderful first anniversary celebration.

8

One World, One Message

The executive committee of the newly formed Slavic Gospel Association strongly believed in sending financial support to areas of greatest need, but only through the supervision of seasoned Christian leaders in those areas. This policy required that Peter travel almost constantly in the early days to fields where Slavic missionaries labored and where pastors and evangelists were in short supply.

He never traveled on purely administrative assignments. Always he combined them with revival meetings. Always he preached. And always the fruits of righteousness followed.

Was he ever inspirationally "dry" before a meeting? "Oh, yes, brother. Dry? You feel like you don't know what you are going to say even as the last hymn is being sung and you're introduced. But then God gives you a message and you start in. You forget even what you announced."

In 1937 the General Director embarked on an extended journey to the Soviet Union, a journey which eventually took him around the world. Travel funds were supplied separately so that nothing was taken from the SGA general fund or missionary reserve.

93

The board of directors urged him to investigate the situation in his homeland one more time, even though they recognized the dangers. Hitler's blitzkreig against Poland was only two years away. Rumors of war were increasing. Pressure against most Soviet citizens in Stalin's Russia was by now intense, yet reports indicated that the Christian faith was alive and vital. Many Christian leaders were being sent to Siberia.

This journey to Russia was Peter's fourth as an evangelist. Some urged him not to go because of the dangers, but on March 22 he left Chicago, his ticket purchased by interested friends for his preaching and fact-finding journey. He also left with the blessing of his brave wife, Vera, who could not help knowing the dangers her husband faced in their homeland. He sailed from New York on the S.S. *Queen Mary* and in four days reached France. Evangelist Deyneka stood out prominently on voyages such as this one. He was usually tapped by the ships' authorities to lead worship services. Out of those casual meetings at sea came lasting friendships and faithful financial supporters of the mission.

Peter disembarked at Cherbourg and took a train for Paris. Letters ahead of the trip had arranged a meeting with Russian believers in the French city at a gospel hall rented for their services.

Geneva . . . Rome . . . then Yugoslavia and through the city of Trieste Peter traveled, finding Russian communities everywhere. His basic themes were the deeper spiritual life, revival, and consecration.

A constant "companion" of Evangelist Deyneka was a tube of garlic-flavored salami. He hung it up in every hotel room in which he slept. Having no sense of smell, Peter could enjoy the taste without the pungent odor that filled every nook and cranny of a furnished room.

Once while visiting England after World War II, when hotel windows were kept tightly shut to conserve heat, he hung up his salami as usual. It was mildewed to a snowy white which Peter simply washed off with cold water. The maid faithfully opened the windows to rid the room of the odor. Peter just as faithfully closed the windows again when he returned.

From Belgrade, Yugoslavia, he traveled to Kishinev, Romania (now Kishinev, USSR), arriving at 3 A.M., to be met by two Christian Jewish brethren who were missionaries among their people in the former Romanian capital. The Jewish brethren took him to various parts of the city on preaching missions. Through this contact, the Slavic Gospel Association had a continuing part in efforts to evangelize the Slavs of that city.

His travel companions through the years recall his absolute insistence on being half an hour early for every train, plane, or meeting.

"I like to leave early so if we have a flat tire or get lost . . ."

Did he ever have a flat tire?

"I wouldn't know what to do if I did, brother! Yes, once in fifty years of traveling to meetings I had a flat tire. It was in the country. That tire exploded so loud it scared us in the car."

Trains were still running on time in Eastern Europe in 1937. From Kishinev, Peter journeyed to Rovno, Poland, two years ahead of the awesome Nazi blitzkreigs. He was met by the Rev. A. Nichiporuk, a pastor-missionary in charge of a large gospel church.

"The Holy Spirit so moved the hearts of people that many souls were saved and believers revived," Peter wrote following his ministry in Poland.

The evangelistic success was all the more remarkable because the city was pelted by driving rain during his entire visit. Bad roads developed, but they could not hinder the gathering crowds.

Kowel was the next city to host the traveling missionary, then Warsaw, and there Peter boarded a train that would carry him to the border of Russia and home to Chomsk.

The moment of parting always rent Peter's heart. Believers were grieved to see him go, bringing to an end the sweet fellowship that Christ promises to those who walk with Him. They strongly warned him not to travel eastward.

"But I *must* go," Peter replied to them as he had done to friends in America who had tried to dissuade him.

They countered with predictions that the moment he stepped over the border the Bolsheviks would arrest him and offer him no way of escape.

"Don't take your Bible!" they advised. "If the Bolsheviks discover you are a Christian they will surely put you in prison."

To each warning Peter simply replied that God was able to protect him from all dangers, and he set his face like a flint to enter his native land.

One Polish man in particular grieved for Peter and his family in America. "I am very sorry for you, Peter," he said repeatedly. "You will have some time getting out of Russia."

Peter looked at him carefully. "Will you pray for me as I go?" he asked.

"Yes," the man promised. "But that will not help."

Peter smiled. *Some encouragement,* he thought.

Christian workers gathered late at night at the Warsaw train depot to see him off and to pray for his safety. They laid their hands on him, committing him to the Lord's care.

The train was filled with Russians and Poles traveling to the last Polish station at Zdowhonovo. Peter rode all night, arriving at the border town at eight the following morning. All the other passengers left the train at Zdowhonovo, leaving him completely alone in the coach.

Feelings of fear and loneliness gripped him. "I recalled all the warnings and the advice of my friends given only the day before," he said as he recalled the harrowing trip. "My

Peter Deyneka attended an evangelical conference in Warsaw, Poland, a short time before the Nazi invasion. Many of these delegates perished in the holocaust of World War II.

Peter pled with American friends to support workers in eastern Europe. Funds that he raised were used to provide bicycles for evangelistic "bicycle brigades."

As war clouds threatened, a great spiritual awakening spread throughout eastern Europe and along the borders of Russia. Many souls were saved in these campaigns and rallies.

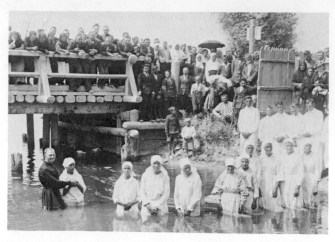

Wherever Peter preached, souls were saved, and many outdoor baptismal services for new converts were the result of this rapid growth.

Border guards were very prominent as Peter Deyneka entered the Soviet Union by train for the long and tedious journey to the Far East on the Trans Siberia Railway.

Believers often came long distances by sled to church. They sat in the hay to keep their feet warm as they traveled.

Completing his trip through Siberia, Peter Deyneka preached in Japan. Even through an interpreter, his sermons were accompanied by strong conviction that fell upon his audience.

thoughts wandered back to America and to my family. Would I see them again?''

At last the train began to move, gaining speed rapidly. He crossed a beautiful land with an abundance of grain, fruit trees, and vegetable farms. Everything was brightly illuminated by the gleaming rays of a golden morning sun. Each mile carried him nearer and nearer to the Soviet border.

As the train sped eastward Peter watched the level terrain grow increasingly less monotonous. Along the railroad bed grew verdant forests, sometimes stretching away in the distance as far as one could see.

In 1930, Peter's mother had received the Lord as her Savior. Her greeting this time would be far different from the weeping and angry tirades that characterized her actions during his first visit home.

Peter found joy in the promises of God. ''They were my only source of comfort,'' he said. ''I could hear them echo through my heart one after another: *Have faith in God . . . only believe . . . I am with you . . . I will never leave thee nor forsake thee . . . call upon me and I will answer thee, and show thee great and mighty things which thou knowest not.*''

Peter resolved in his heart that he would not fear what man would do to him. ''My Bible shall go with me!'' he decided.

As he gazed through the open windows of the train he saw in the distance two high posts marking the Russian gateway across the border. The train began to slow down. Peter lifted his trembling heart to God in prayer.

Soviet Russia! All doors and windows were closed. The train became stuffy and hot. A Soviet officer stepped inside Peter's car and called, ''Pozhalusta vash pasport'' (Your passport, please).

Peter fished into his pocket and drew out the precious document.

The officer took it, saying, ''You will get it back at Shepetovka'' (the Russian customshouse).

An hour later the train arrived at the customshouse where

100

Peter was ordered to open his baggage. An Intourist interpreter who knew English spoke to him in Russian.

A militia man and woman asked him to open his suitcase. Peter obliged. The first thing that fell out was his Bible. He took it and with trembling hands gave it to the customs officer. The official looked it over and laid it aside, inspecting more closely other items in the luggage. "Close it up," he said.

Hallelujah! Peter sang in his heart. *My Bible is going with me!*

The woman officer counted his money and gave him a receipt. She also registered the camera with his passport. "You must show this receipt when you leave the country," she explained. "Without it you will not be allowed to take your money out of Russia."

By 2:00 P.M. Peter was processed and ready to enter the country. The midsummer heat was almost unbearable but Peter noticed he was shaking from fear. The year was 1937 and Russia was still in the murderous grip of Stalin's purges.

A few moments after repacking his suitcase Peter was speeding southward on an express train toward Baku. In the dining car he ate his first meal in Soviet Russia—a bowl of Ukrainian *borscht,* several slices of bread with butter, and a bottle of lemonade. While Peter was still inside the train at the Kiev depot, a Russian Jew working for the Intourist Department picked up his luggage and greeted him by name. The stranger announced he would be his guide during his stopover.

An automobile was waiting at the station which took Peter directly to a tourist hotel in the large Russian city. As a tourist, Peter was treated to an exceptionally delicious supper. He noticed that the streets were clean, that clothing was expensive, and that the people were dressed simply but neatly.

On Sunday morning Peter wanted to find a Russian gospel church, but his guide desired to take him to a shoe factory.

"We have plenty of shoes in America," Peter told his guide. "I am interested in seeing churches in Russia."

He was given permission to search for one. The guide had boasted that "a good many" churches were open in Kiev. He did not think Peter would have difficulty finding one.

"Go ahead and try to find one if you want to go to church to say your prayers."

Peter replied, "I could say my prayers in the hotel room, but I want to see how the people worship in Protestant churches as well as in the Orthodox churches."

"Why?" the guide demanded. "Are you interested in religion?"

"Yes," Peter explained, "because I am a Bible believer. I believe in the Lord Jesus Christ as my Savior."

His guide shrugged.

Peter searched in vain for a church that Sunday morning. But he had in his pocket the addresses of some Christian brethren whom he visited instead. Through them he found a gospel church.

Peter noticed that several ministers were seated on the platform that evening. They appeared to him "very poor and very thin," for indeed some had recently returned from years of exile.

One of the preachers stood up to greet the congregation. "Dear brothers and sisters, let us thank God for this wonderful opportunity we have to get together once more to worship our Lord Jesus Christ," the pastor said. "He is worthy of praise. Let us pray."

Many in the room knelt; others remained standing as is the custom in Russian evangelical churches. With one voice the Christians opened their hearts and prayed. The intercession continued for fifteen minutes. Tears ran down the faces of many as they thanked God for the privilege of speaking to Him in prayer.

Vigorous singing followed. The songs "came from the depths of their hearts and throbbed with earnestness," Peter noted. "One songbook was shared by five, sometimes ten people. Most sang from memory."

Three men preached that night in a service that lasted for three hours. The closing speaker took his text from Romans 10:13, "Whosoever shall call upon the name of the Lord shall be saved."

While the service was in progress Peter noticed several uniformed Russian soldiers standing in the congregation. They were listening with great interest, convincing Peter that the gospel had not lost its power in a land which had declared itself officially atheistic.

Peter's heart was stirred by a desire to preach "the wonderful gospel so powerful everywhere in any land and in any culture."

In a season of prayer at the close, Peter noticed that even the soldiers bowed their heads in reverence as sinners cried out to God for mercy.

He wrote home that he was "thoroughly convinced that people in Russia are hungry for the gospel of Jesus Christ."

When the service had ended, a couple was united in marriage by the preacher of the evangelical Christian church. They had sat on one of the few seats during the service and stepped forward as the preacher announced, *"Sey-chas budyem eemet brakosochetanie"* ("We will now proceed with the marriage").

The entire congregation strained to see as the young bride and groom knelt before the minister. The couple stood as the minister admonished them to live a holy married life. The choir sang several hymns suitable for the occasion ("God, Give Them Happiness" and "Two Hands Before God"). They knelt and prayed again until the pastor pronounced the benediction and invited the gathered friends to greet the young couple.

Some churches in Kiev—including Baptist, Evangelical, Lutheran, and Russian Orthodox, had as many as four services each week. They met in simple, unadorned halls, for the ornate Greek Orthodox monasteries had been closed since 1930. No longer could the faithful make their pilgrimages, walking sometimes thousands of miles to say their prayers under the gold-plated domes.

The great churches were now used as antireligion museums where students and tourists were shown the relics of various religions which had flourished in their country before communism was introduced.

During his visit to one of these museums in Kiev, Peter was guided through many underground tunnels where he saw collections of sacred objects which had been kept by the monks and worshiped by the weary pilgrims. Peter took his tour on Monday, the Russian day of rest at that time. Clusters of children, out of school for the day, mingled with him on the tour. They heard lectures in which God and religion were criticized and impudently railed at.

An early-morning express train on Tuesday took Peter overnight to Moscow. His Intourist guide failed to meet his train at 11:00 A.M., leaving Peter puzzled concerning his next move.

An hour passed before he could determine where he should go and what he should do. Finally, the communist chief of the station called a taxi and worked out the details of his Moscow visit.

"It pays to travel with God!" Peter wrote. "Jesus is the best Friend you can have in this world."

He said the same thing in Leningrad and across the Soviet Union on the trans-Siberian express train bound for Otpor, Siberia, and the Manchurian border. He traveled on to Tientsin and Shanghai in China and thence to Japan.

The Japanese gave Peter some trying moments following his arrival to speak at a meeting of Russian believers in Tokyo.

The phone rang in his room at approximately 5:00 P.M. A man speaking English was calling from the front desk: "Mr. Deyneka?"

"Yes."

"You are required to appear at the police headquarters at

ten o'clock tomorrow morning. They want to talk to you."

"Police?" Peter asked, astonished. "What do they want me for?"

"Well," the voice said, "I don't know, but you must go there."

"How do they know I'm here?" Peter asked. "I just arrived!"

"I don't know," the voice replied.

"But I am an American citizen. Do they want to see my passport?"

"No, they want to see *you*!"

Peter began pacing the room. *Here I am,* he thought, *after traveling all through Europe, Siberia, and China without any trouble and in Tokyo police want to arrest me!*

Instead of sleeping that night he spent the hours praying hard for the Lord's protection. The following morning Peter took a taxi and went to the police headquarters. The chief questioned Peter extensively on where he had been and why he had come to Japan, writing down each answer in detail. For three and a half hours the evangelist answered pointed questions, not knowing the reason for the grilling.

"How did you know I was in Tokyo?" he finally asked.

The police explained that a pastor of one of the churches in which he had arranged to speak had informed the police that the Russian-born visitor would be in his pulpit.

"We will be in church to hear you," the Japanese promised.

Several officers afterward took Peter to a cafe, where they bought him tea and continued to ask questions until they were satisfied with his report.

As had been the case in dozens of other cities, Peter's sermons were accompanied by strong conviction which fell upon his audience. The pastor asked the people to remain after the service and pray. Most of them did, bursting forth in spontaneous praise and prayer.

As Peter left the service that evening a police officer met him at a side door.

"I have something for you, Reverend Deyneka," he said, holding out to the visitor a large, beautiful bouquet of flowers. "Please accept these as a token from the police force of Tokyo. We sincerely hope that you will come again."

Peter carried the flowers with him on the train to Yokohama where he boarded a ship bound for Seattle, reserving the last berth on a small vessel. He left only a few days before war broke out between China and Japan. He had circled the world and found Russians in every city he visited.

Missionaries sponsored by the Slavic Gospel Association would eventually follow Peter to those fields and beyond, in quest of trophies of grace among his people.

The following year he established work among Russian-Aleuts. The Russians had discovered and populated Alaska's Aleutian Island in the mid-1700s. Peter found in Alaska Russian-Aleuts with names like Stepanoff and Osbekoff. Their ancestors had intermarried years before with Russian fur traders and began following Russian customs. These Russian-speaking Aleuts had a knowledge of church ritualism but few had heard of the gospel of Jesus Christ.

In the spring of 1939 the Slavic Gospel Association's first North American missionary, Walter Covich, heard the challenge of missions in the northland and established a witness among the Russian-speaking Aleuts. This ministry grew to sponsor twenty missionaries in eight locations working in one of the world's most remote areas.

That same year Peter Deyneka traveled to Cuba, and in 1940 to the continent of South America which opened wide to the Slavic Gospel Association's ministries to Russians—a rapidly expanding mission to a rapidly expanding mission field on the move.

King Cove—a typical Aleutian fishing village where
SGA missionaries have taken the gospel.

Peter Deyneka was challenged by the spiritual needs of the Russians
who remained in Alaska, but there are many unreached Aleuts, Es-
kimos, and Indians.

Missionary statesman Dr. Oswald J. Smith with Peter Deyneka. Dr. Smith spoke at this S.G.A workers conference in Alaska.

Today, precious Alaskan children in remote villages hear that Jesus loves them.

9

South to the Harvest

Two years after circling the globe with one message about one faith for one world, Peter Deyneka in 1940 turned his attention to Russians living in the fourth largest continent—South America.

The continent is nearly twice the size of the United States, offering the Russian evangelist "twice the blessing," which he described in a booklet titled *Revival in South America*.

Workers in the Slavic Gospel Association prepared for Peter's trip by praying specifically that if he were to open a ministry to Russians settled in Latin America, enough gifts designated for such a trip would be contributed.

By November 1940, his round-trip ticket was purchased, and a farewell meeting arranged in the Russian Evangelical Christian Church of Chicago. Peter sailed from New York on the S.S. *Brazil* with his Russian Bible and a heart full of faith.

On the first Sunday at sea, the ship's captain asked him to conduct divine services in the first-class section for all passengers aboard.

"I could not say No," Peter admitted, "because I had

promised the Lord that I would be ready anytime and anywhere—even on the sea—to witness for Him."

After the service the captain asked the enthusiastic Russian preacher to direct the remaining two services of the voyage. Peter enlisted Mr. Ream of Cleveland, Ohio, to assist him in reading the Scriptures and praying. Mrs. Ream organized a men's chorus which sang two numbers.

Seventeen days after leaving New York the ship docked at Rio de Janeiro, where Peter boarded a train for Sao Paulo (which was then the capital) to meet his first Russian and Ukrainian fellow-believers in South America.

"There is immediate need for a trained Russian Christian worker here," Peter wrote home. "Pray!"

A Russian brother took him three hundred miles inland to visit Russian colonies in Uruguay. The land the Europeans farmed could only be rented for seven years in one place. Consequently he found his people living in mud houses with tin roofs. When the seven years were up they destroyed their homes, took the tin roofs with them and moved to another place to remain for another seven years.

Peter's meetings were held in such temporary homes. "People here are hungry for the Word of God," he said.

At a train station farther into Uruguay, Peter was met by the leader of an evangelical Christian church and by three other brethren. He arrived at the beginning of harvest. By horse and wagon he rumbled over dirt roads through fields of golden wheat, arriving eventually at the humble home of his Russian host. Inside, a group of neighbors had gathered and eagerly welcomed Peter to their farming community.

Word of a visiting Russian "kinsman" traveled fast, and quickly the lane was dotted with Russians on foot and in wagons, making their way to the house gathering where Peter opened his Russian Bible to expound to hungry hearts the life-giving message.

His travel diary records the results: "Hearts were melted, believers revived, backsliders reclaimed, sinners converted.

Thank God for this great hunger for the Bread of Life.''

In a few days the farmers became Peter's devoted friends. He found it difficult to break away when the time came to depart for Argentina.

''The love of Christ has bound us together,'' Peter told the Russian settlers in Uruguay.

A contingent of them left the harvest to accompany him to the train station in Paysandu to send him on his missionary journey southward. Many wept. ''We had waited for such a long time for your coming,'' they told him. ''Now you must leave so soon?''

As Peter surveyed the crowd of humble Russian peasant farmers he could not assume they would ever meet again on this earth. But he determined in his heart that he would continue the fellowship with them through the long arms of prayer.

A train took him to the eastern coast where he boarded a ship for Buenos Aires.

As he stepped from the gangplank, Peter quickly realized that there would be difficulties in his preaching mission to Argentina.

''You are to come with us, Brother Deyneka!'' a group of believers called.

''No!'' another group insisted. ''You must come with us!''

Peter was unable to determine who were his true hosts. ''Please, let me first get my baggage,'' he said, holding up his hands for quiet. ''I will try to visit you all.''

The American visitor checked his notebook and sought out the party with whom he had corresponded about the meetings. It was agreed that he would go with him and his party first, then preach to the other group later.

''Many who came from Europe ten or twelve years earlier have fallen into a backslidden condition,'' Peter wrote home. ''There is no one to lead them. I have found coldness and bitterness. But, thank God, there were a few who had faithfully been praying for many years that a spiritual revival would visit their people."

The missionary discovered that some of these people now living in Argentina he had met while they were still in Poland. To several he had given New Testaments which they still carried with them.

By night Peter preached in scheduled services; by day he met a stream of discouraged and defeated people hoping to find deliverance from their problems. Sometimes he counseled with people from 9:00 A.M. until after midnight.

One Russian service stands out boldly in the Deyneka South American diary—a service in a Spanish Baptist Church in Buenos Aires where the Russians held their meetings each Lord's Day. The memorable service began shortly after supper and lasted until midnight.

"What crying out to God!" Peter wrote. "The people confessed sins to one another, praised God for the Holy Spirit, and rejoiced in the spiritual renewal which had swept through their church."

Nobody wanted to go home. Men embraced each other, sometimes with tears, as they asked forgiveness for hard feelings. Then they prayed some more, giving thanks to God.

"I cannot describe to you what took place in this meeting," Peter said. "As we were on our knees praising God, two brethren whispered to me that they must go to another community where there were Russian families who needed God."

These men left immediately and reached their destination at 1:00 A.M. As they entered the first house they shouted, "Everybody get up! God is working in the church. Great miracles have happened. Get up! Get right with God and with each other."

A lady of the house at once got out of bed and began to weep and pray to God. Then the visitors went to another house, calling on their friends to rouse themselves from sleep in order to enjoy the renewing that God had brought to their stale, tried, and troubled assembly.

In a third house three families gathered in one room for prayer, repenting and asking God not to pass them by.

"We did not sleep all night," the brethren said to Peter in the morning after they returned from their journey. "We spent all our time praying for the Russian people of South America."

The strain of travel, all-day counseling, and extensive preaching drained Peter of physical strength. But in the midst of it he testified that "my heart was overflowing with joy." Each time he looked into the face of a Russian he felt an overpowering urge to make certain that person had made his peace with God.

One of those faces belonged to a man in obvious misery. The Russian had migrated to South America eleven years earlier, leaving his wife and their son. In the New World he had fallen into sin, forgetting his family.

When Peter was in Russia in 1937 he had met the wife of this man. She had begged him to help find her husband in South America, and now in a gospel service Peter was preaching to him.

Part of the way through the sermon he sent a note to the preacher asking Peter to pray for him immediately. The note also asked the entire congregation to unite in prayer for him.

"I let the man struggle a while longer under his conviction," Peter stated. "I felt he needed the extra time to let God speak to him."

During the rest of Peter's talk the man was weeping continuously. When Peter closed the meeting with an invitation to Christians to surrender their lives to God, people started to stream toward the altar. Some almost ran. Many were in tears. The presence of the Lord filled the tiny church where even atheists and strangers had gathered.

No one left for two hours. The man who had left his family in Russia wept as though his heart had broken under the weight of conviction.

When the praying was quieted, the man asked if he could speak to the church. He went to the front of the room, but he was so broken he could not speak for a long while. Finally his story began to spill out. He warned his friends how terrible it is to be a backslider, drifting away from God and living in sin.

"Please forgive me," he said. "Pray for me."

After the service the man came to Peter and explained, "Brother Deyneka, I feel like a new man! A great burden has left my heart, but I am so sorry that I wasted my life in sin these past eleven years in South America."

Later the repentant Russian wrote out his testimony and had it printed. "I can boldly testify before all what the Lord has done for me," he wrote. "I can now truly say that in my heart I feel the presence of the Holy Spirit. Great joy has filled my heart. For this I constantly thank my Lord that He, through brother Deyneka, took me out of the miry clay. Now I can say *Hallelujah!*

"This experience has been the joy of many others also. . . ."

The testimony included special thanks to friends of the Slavic Gospel Association who made it possible for Peter Deyneka to visit that obscure church for such far-reaching and significant results.

One result of the revival in Buenos Aires was the uniting of the two separated groups who had fought over the sponsorship of the missionary when he first arrived. As one body they officially asked Peter's mission to send a trained gospel worker to lead their united church.

In Buenos Aires, Hebrew missionary Paul Rosenberg invited Peter to speak in his Hebrew Christian Mission—the only such mission in South America at that time. Peter also addressed a group of Christian businessmen from London,

England, preaching in a beautiful new YWCA building to an English-speaking audience. He also spoke at a Spanish Baptist church with an American missionary interpreting.

The welcome of Russians in South America was warm and enthusiastic, and their farewells were tearful and full of singing. Another "unforgettable" event (and there were many thus recorded by Peter on this voyage) was the farewell he received in Buenos Aires, arranged by believers who had been blessed by his preaching. Among the group assembled were three Russian communists, but they did not escape the finger of God.

Thirty-seven Russians gathered around singing as Peter climbed aboard the train. He opened the window of the car and offered a prayer just as the train began to move.

"Come back soon and stay longer, Brother Deyneka," someone shouted.

The train sped on toward the province of Misiones, Argentina. Peter watched one flat field after another approach and disappear. More than fifty thousand Russian and Ukrainian people lived in Misiones Province. Most of them had come to Argentina a decade earlier. They had found only a few Indians living on the territory. With the free land given them by the Argentine government the Russian farmers cleared out the timber and fought to clear the land for crops. Before the land began to produce, the pioneers endured great poverty. They cut roads through the fields of red clay, but the least amount of rain turned them into impossible sloughs of mud.

On one trip, as Peter bounced along on a twelve-mile journey by horse and wagon, he often had to get out and help the horse pull the wagon through the ruts. But the roads dried quickly with small amounts of sunshine, bringing to vivid color the beautiful orchards of banana, orange, and lemon trees.

Although the people—both poor pioneer and affluent established farmer—were all thankful not to be in Europe, they

A crowded church in Sao Paulo, Brazil, where revival broke out. As Peter Deyneka preached, strong men broke down under deep conviction and wept in repentance.

Some Slavic colonies in the jungles of South America were so isolated that no roads reached them. One time when Peter Deyneka and his party forded a flood-swollen stream, their wagon was almost swept away.

Peter Deyneka recognized the need for more Slavic workers to reap the ready harvest of souls in South America and pled with American Christians to support dedicated workers such as these men.

People gathered from miles around to hear the fiery evangelist from America. Sometimes two or three congregations would come together for several days of meetings.

did not forget to build their log prayer houses where they could gather to worship.

In Misiones, heat and humidity plagued the traveler, but the revival meetings went on. Many people walked to the meetings, coming from all parts of the province. A spirit of repentance and deep searching after God characterized the meetings, just as they always had from the time Peter Deyneka began to preach the gospel. Summer fruits and grain had to be harvested, but the people made time to come hear the evangelist.

"When they saw Christians revived," Peter noted, "it was no trouble for the unsaved to come to Christ."

The moderator announced in one service that Peter would be preaching next in a gospel mission twenty-five miles away. So many people wanted to attend meetings that the church had to rent a bus. Still others traveled by horseback, and many walked the day's journey to the chapel.

Peter rode in the bus, arriving hot and tired at 9:00 A.M. to begin the meeting with prayer.

"I felt the presence of God as I began to speak," he said. "I noticed people weeping. Some even cried out loud, making it difficult for me to continue my message. The revival was on!"

Peter urged his people to obey the Holy Spirit "whatever the need may be in your life." At once people fell down on their knees and began to cry out to God. A lady who had been expelled from the church for backsliding came under deep conviction. This woman's family had planted tobacco—a revulsion to the Russian believers who are strongly against the use of tobacco and the earning of money from it. The tobacco growers prospered financially, but they had lost the joy of their fellowship with the Russian Christian community.

That day the woman prayed that God could take all her riches and possessions, but that she wanted back the assurance and happiness of her salvation.

Another backslider who had been expelled from the

church cried out, "Oh God, I am left out; I have lost my fellowship with Thee and with my brothers and sisters in Christ."

While this prayer was being offered a man rushed up to Peter from the back of the church. He threw his arms around Peter's neck and cried out, "I want to be saved . . . I want to be saved . . . I want to be saved!"

Both men knelt—the convicted man offering the sinner's prayer which Peter taught him to pray.

For some moments the tempest of holy revival continued, sweeping away hard feelings and restoring unity and power to the small congregation of farmers.

Peter asked the choir to sing, but they too were under such conviction that they could not finish the selection through their weeping and sobbing. This reaction by a church choir occurred in several other places visited by Peter in areas of South America.

Peter conducted four meetings that day. At the last evening session "fifteen unsaved people rushed to the altar for salvation," while many others throughout the congregation wept. People did not want to return to their farms. Three times Peter told them the meeting was over and begged them to go home. But nobody would move. They wanted to go on.

"Brother," someone cried out, "please tell us some more and let us pray again." The Russians seemed to be prepared to stay all night.

An area-wide revival service was planned for Sunday morning in the largest church of the district. Three choirs would join to provide the music. The service would be a farewell meeting for Peter. Rain fell steadily all day Saturday and the roads became more rutted and treacherous.

"We had stayed so long in the church all day Saturday that nobody wanted to go home," Peter reported. "I suggested that before they end the meeting, we all pray and ask God to stop the rain at least until noon on Sunday, if it was His will that we have the farewell gathering."

After the prayer the rain stopped abruptly. Early Sunday

morning a hot sun appeared to dry out the roads. Two trucks transported the choir members to the appointed place twenty-five miles away.

The weather remained beautiful until 1:00 P.M. on Sunday afternoon. Just as the service ended, suddenly dark clouds hid the sun and rain fell in a cloudburst.

"Brother Deyneka," people chided, "why didn't you pray that there would be no rain for all day?"

They had to transport their guest through three miles of rain-soaked mud roads to a German Baptist church. When Peter arrived so many people had gathered that there was no room for a great crowd of latecomers outside.

Again Peter's preaching was met by stirring revival in which sinners repented of their iniquity, backsliders were reclaimed, and enemies reunited in friendship.

The mission to Misiones ended with a baptismal service for the newly converted, following a side trip to a colony where ten thousand Ukrainians had settled.

Paraguay was next on Peter's South American preaching and fact-finding circuit. Here also, thousands of Slavic immigrants had settled. Up the Paraguay River Peter sailed, thence twenty-five miles into the hinterland with a delegation of five Russian brethren from as many provinces. They had come a day early so they wouldn't miss his arrival.

Peter was hot and tired, but he dared not disappoint his hosts. The midsummer heat wilted him quickly, but there was no respite for the visiting preacher. Traveling sometimes on two-wheeled wagons, periodically on foot, and occasionally by horseback, Peter found hungry hearts wherever he went. His hands and ankles were badly bitten by tiny insects, and loss of sleep had weakened him, but there was no complaining.

"My heart was full of joy and praise to God for the privilege I had to be among these hungry souls," he said.

By train Peter journeyed back to Argentina, arriving in a little town about six o'clock at night. A cluster of Russian and Ukrainian people met him. Should he leave immediately for the gathered congregation? Or should he remain to speak to the crowd who had met him and imploringly urged him to conduct a gospel meeting?

After much confusion he told the brother who had come to escort him that he would not be in the meeting until the following morning. But instead of leaving to inform the church that Peter would not be coming, the brother remained in the group to hear the visitor preach.

Once, Peter stopped and reminded him to go tell the people.

"Don't worry, Brother Deyneka," he said. "They won't leave until I get there."

Peter decided the man's soul was so hungry he wanted to get all he could for himself.

A four-wheeled wagon drawn by horses took him the next day to a clearing in the woods. It was hot, and Peter had rested only fitfully the night before.

As soon as he stepped off the wagon the leader presented him to the waiting crowd of people: "Here is our brother, for whom we have been waiting."

Peter prayed that God would supply strength. He chose as his theme "Full Surrender to Christ." After he had spoken thirty minutes the conviction which had characterized his earlier meetings fell on the people. Men, women, and children stood enthralled, listening until Peter's strength and time were gone. He called for prayer and sat down. Earnest Christians among the people began to pray with him. One of the men hurried to the platform. "Brother Deyneka," he whispered, "won't you stay longer?"

Peter shook his head. "I'm sorry," he replied. "I must go to other places. If I had my way I would remain." In his heart he determined to raise up workers in the United States to be missionaries to these new friends.

From the rural woodland of Argentina Peter traveled to Tumoca, Chile, for meetings arranged by workers of the

Christian and Missionary Alliance. Finally he traveled north to Quito, Ecuador, at the invitation of Mr. and Mrs. Clarence Jones, pioneer missionaries who founded Radio Station HCJB. This stopover became historic for Peter. At a casual invitation by Mr. Jones, he broadcast the gospel in the Russian language on history's first program of good news beamed by shortwave to Russian-speaking people. This broadcast was heard by Mrs. Deyneka in far-off Chicago on a shortwave set. It was to be the first of many thousands of Russian gospel broadcasts sent out by the Slavic Gospel Association in cooperation with various missionary radio stations.

A brief stop in Havana, Cuba, completed Peter's mission, bringing him home to an intensive recruitment campaign for workers in the South American harvest.

10

The School That Prayer Built

As Peter Deyneka charted his global travels among Slavic peoples he longed to raise up an army of trained Christian workers to win his scattered countrymen for Jesus Christ.

Lenin and Stalin were busily training workers in Russian communism, but there was no program of Biblical instruction for Slavic Christian young people. The words of the apostle Paul burned in Peter's heart: "How shall they believe in him of whom they have not heard? And how shall they hear without a preacher?"

No Bible-training institution in the world offered pastoral courses for Russian-speaking young people or served the cultural needs of this segment of youth. The time was right to open such a school. But where? How?

In 1943, two years after Peter returned from South America, he arranged to meet Pastor Oswald J. Smith of Peoples Church in Toronto, Canada. Dr. Smith had made his first visit to Russia in 1924 at the age of thirty-four. In 1929 Dr. Smith went again to the borders of Russia, and in 1936 he made his third trip to Russia. He wrote several magazine articles reporting on his experiences. These stirred the imagination of the Canadian and American public as he wrote of eager Russian listeners, crowded meetings, fervent prayer sessions, and overwhelming responses to the invitation. By the time Peter approached him to discuss the need for a Bible Institute to train Russian workers, both pastor and congregation at the Peoples Church were ready for a united effort.

In 1943, the first classes of the Russian Bible Institute opened in a large room of the educational building of Peoples Church. Forty-five students enrolled, taught by four professors. The program was a three-year Bible course with all the basics such as Bible doctrine, personal evangelism, church history, homiletics, Christian education, pastoral training, missions, hermeneutics, Old and New Testament introduction, and other subjects.

All lessons were taught in the Russian language. Besides classroom conversation, the grammar, vocabulary, and phonetics of the Russian language were taught to help students improve their use of the mother tongue. For the students who had grown up in a country foreign to their ancestry, Russian literature, culture, and history were necessary subjects.

The burgeoning city of Toronto accommodated a large Slavic population among which the students could conduct personal evangelism door-to-door, in the parks, and on the street corners.

In the mid-1940s, following the devastation of World War II, multiplied thousands of Slavic refugees and displaced persons poured into Canada from the settlement camps of Germany, Austria, and Czechoslovakia. Many settled in Toronto, bringing to the doorstep of students at RBI a new and responsive mission field. Most of the immigrants had escaped from Slavic countries where atheism had been taught to them daily. Now at last they were free to hear the gospel, to attend churches, to teach their children about God and the Bible. As a result, children of these refugees began enrolling in the Russian Bible Institute to prepare for Christian service.

The unique annual missionary conferences at Peoples Church exposed the students to a global missionary program that was available in few churches in America and Canada. Many responded as Dr. Smith and Rev. Deyneka shared their vision.

In seven years, the Russian Bible Institute graduated eighty-five well-trained, dedicated Russian young people. Most were commissioned for full-time Christian service in South America, Korea, the Philippine Islands, Europe, Canada, and the United States.

In February 1944, some of the Slavic Gospel Association missionaries in Argentina formed a committee to seek the best location for a second Russian Bible Institute like the one functioning in Toronto.

A large, old building in Rosario, Argentina, was selected as the facility in which to launch the project. God raised up teachers for each position in the new school: deans, librarians, cooks, and other personnel. All lent their support to the Argentine school, which in due time replaced Canada's experiment in Christian education among Slavic young people. Now the South American school has become the world's only Russian Bible Institute, replacing the Toronto pioneering venture in 1950.

The earliest workers in the new school in Argentina were recruited from Peter's home city, Chicago. These young people from Russian churches of Chicago were challenged by Peter to enlist their services for missions. Many were trained at Moody Bible Institute and went on to work in Alaska, Europe, Australia, and South America.

Two of the Slavic young people in the Chicago team were Constantine Lewshenia and Mary Beechick. Mary was first to respond to the call for workers in South America. She sailed for Argentina. About a year later, Const also left for South America, together with Sam Fewchuk, a Ukrainian from Canada whose life had been influenced by Peter Deyneka.

"Why don't you stop at HCJB in Quito and give a hand with the Russian radio broadcasts?" Peter suggested. So Const's first assignment was at a microphone addressing millions of fellow Slavs in Europe and the Americas. Sam went on to Argentina where he did two things: he married Mary Beechick, whom he had met in Chicago, and became one of the founders of the Russian Bible Institute in Rosario.

A fourth member of the Chicago team, Russia-born Elizabeth Zernov, heard God's call to South America. Elizabeth, with four sisters, two brothers, and their parents, had miraculously escaped from Russia in the 1930s to settle in Beaver Dam, Wisconsin. Peter Deyneka's abundant enthusiasm and vision reached that home. In time, four of the talented Zernov daughters became workers and missionaries with the Slavic Gospel Association.

Elizabeth's first assignment was in Quito to help organize the Russian department of the global broadcasts dispatched daily by Radio Station HCJB. She came by plane—unlike Const, Sam, and Mary, who had taken the hard way to the mission field, enduring lengthy boat travel and arduous train trips through the Andes Mountains. Const and Elizabeth became better acquainted in Quito and fell in love. By the time Const left for Argentina they were engaged.

The end of March 1944, arrived. It was time to open the Rosario school. Only a few applications were in hand. Would there be enough students for a school?

A few days before opening on April 1, more students began to arrive. Many brought their application forms with them instead of mailing them on ahead. Others came with friends who had not bothered to fill out application forms.

Twenty-six students enrolled that first year. In 1945 the Rev. Moses Gitlin, prominent Russian Hebrew-Christian, arrived from the Russian Bible Institute in Toronto to assist in preparation of curriculum and in teaching at the newly

First student body of the Russian Bible Institute in Toronto, Canada —the school built upon prayer and the vision of men such as Dr. Oswald J. Smith and Peter Deyneka.

The present building of the Russian Bible Institute in Temperley, a suburb of Buenos Aires, Argentina, was purchased by faith for fifteen thousand dollars. The Lord supplied these funds through one American saint of God.

Students at the Russian Bible Institute in Argentina come from all over South America and from as far away as North America and Australia.

At the Russian Bible Institute, the only one in the world, all classes are in the Russian language.

established school. Gitlin came via Quito. There Elizabeth Zernov joined him for the journey to Argentina where her fiancé Const had patiently waited for twenty-two months. Thirteen days after he arrived in Argentina, Professor Gitlin united Const and Elizabeth in holy matrimony.

During vacations and holidays, the student body scattered to the backwoods of Argentina to put into practical use the lessons they had learned. The faculty joined them as the Fewchuks, Lewshenias, and Professor Gitlin traveled throughout Uruguay, Paraguay, Argentina, and into Brazil to minister to Slavic colonies. They also recruited students for RBI.

Because the Slavic community in South America remained a minority, the student body was never large. Sometimes the count went to forty, but each student was seriously committed to missionary work. An average of 85 percent of each class stepped out into active Christian service.

Const and Elizabeth eventually returned to Radio Station HCJB. Sam and Mary Fewchuk went to pioneer areas of Australia. But God raised up new teachers and workers as the Russian Bible Institute expanded its influence among new and larger Slavic communities. Eventually a building in Temperley, Buenos Aires, was found for fifteen thousand dollars and purchased by faith. In April 1956, it was opened and continues to be the headquarters of the world's only Russian Bible Institute.

In 1956—the year RBI opened in Temperley—Andrew and Pauline Semenchuk arrived. For twelve years Andrew directed the school, launching evening classes and special classes to train lay leaders of the Russian evangelical churches in Buenos Aires in addition to the regular curriculum.

Andrew was born in Russia, but came to Canada with his parents at the age of four. Peter Deyneka's frequent visits to the little country church which the Semenchuks attended made a lasting impression on the young man. Andrew was among the first to eagerly enroll in the first class of the Russian Bible Institute in Toronto.

Meanwhile, Peter Deyneka's influence reached another Slavic home in Chicago to touch the life of Pauline Mazur. This daughter of a Russian Orthodox priest had a godly mother who eventually won her husband to the Lord Jesus Christ. Pauline, too, was enrolled at RBI in Toronto where she met Andrew. After their graduation and marriage, they returned to Chicago where Andrew finished seminary training and prepared himself for ministries in Europe, Alaska, and South America. He is today Assistant Director of the Slavic Gospel Association.

The yearbooks of the Russian Bible Institutes are filled with an honor roll of stalwart Slavic pioneer missionaries in many countries.

Two of the Institutes' notable students were the Deynekas' eldest daughter Ruth, and her husband, Jack Shalanko. They met first as students in Toronto. In 1950 Ruth went to Europe to serve the Lord among Slavic people in Germany and France. After his graduation from the Russian Bible Institute in Toronto, Jack went to Trieste, Italy, where he worked among the ten thousand refugees in the displaced persons camps of Trieste.

It was here that Jack and Ruth met again. After their marriage in 1953, they went to South America, where they have found a fruitful ministry at the microphones of HCJB, ministering to Russian people around the world. Jack carries on a Bible Conference ministry in English as well as in Spanish.

Jack Koziol was born in the Ukraine and raised in Canada. Upon graduation from RBI, he and his wife, Vera, began their ministry among Slavic immigrants in Canada. Later they directed Slavic ministries to Russia at Radio Station HLKX, owned by the Evangelical Alliance Mission in South Korea. They now direct broadcasts to Russia at Far East Broadcasting Company's complex in the Philippines.

The doctrines Jack learned at RBI are now being transmitted by radio to faithful men and women throughout Central Russia.

Roza Kucher stepped from the graduation platform into the turmoil of postwar Europe, sharing the gospel among the several million Russian displaced persons after World War II.

While in Europe "Roz" met missionary Nick Leonovich whom she later married. Together they now evangelize Russia as Slavic Gospel Association missionaries through the facilities of Trans World Radio in Monte Carlo, Monaco.

Alex. Kuvshinikov was born in Russia and became a Christian in Pennsylvania. He enrolled at RBI in Argentina where he met Elodia, a Russian from Paraguay, who became his wife. Their mission field to Slavic people was first in Seoul, South Korea, at missionary Radio Station HLKX. Alex sent the message of Jesus Christ into Siberia—the very area where his uncle was once imprisoned under Josef Stalin for the gospel's sake. Now the Kuvshinikovs continue their Russian radio ministry from HCJB.

Basilio Polischuk entered the Russian Bible Institute to learn how to witness more effectively among forgotten Russians living in a Spanish culture . . . working in meat packing factories . . . drinking themselves into blurred forgetfulness.

Today Basilio, his wife Zina, and their four children live among those disadvantaged Russians, distributing God's Word, pointing young and old to joy and happiness through faith in Jesus Christ.

Typical of still other graduates from the Russian Bible Institute are Mary and Nicolas Slobodian. These devoted missionaries preach to Argentine Russians from the sun-baked cotton fields to the bustling cities.

In the course of their ministry their lives have been threatened, as was the case when they met the drunken Russian husband of a faithful parishioner.

"If you baptize my wife I'll kill you and her too!" he raged against Mary and Nicolas.

For several months the Slobodians had driven twenty kilometers (12½ miles) every week through the hot fields to visit Russian families living in remote Slavic colonies. In one sad home they had met Mrs. K and her alcoholic husband.

At first Mr. K was intrigued by the Bible message of hope which he had never heard before. Then the K's son, daughter-in-law, and their eleven children who lived on a farm four kilometers (about 2½ miles) from the gospel meeting all came to hear Nicolas preach.

Their son's family was also in great need. Like his father, the son was an alcoholic. His large family lived in a bedraggled two-room adobe shelter and barely subsisted on a few acres of neglected land. But as the Slobodians visited repeatedly, the son came to the Lord and was cleansed of sin and of his tragic habit.

Gradually the entire family came to the Lord—except the father. He continued to rage at his Christian wife and beat her repeatedly. Many nights she slept in the woods to escape his wrath.

Despite her husband's threats, she insisted that she must be baptized. "Even if I only live a day or two I want to be baptized," Mrs. K told her husband.

Reluctantly, the Slobodians finally agreed to baptize the determined new convert, her son, daughter-in-law, and their eleven children. Aware of the danger from the father, the new converts and the Slobodians prepared for the baptism. Mr. K also made preparations to carry out his threats.

The day of the baptisms came. Stayed by the hand of the Lord, and perhaps by conviction at the sight of so many of his family following the Lord, Mr. K hung at the edge of the crowd which had gathered for the baptism. He did no harm as his family entered the waters of baptism.

The Slobodians are still traveling the twenty kilometers over nearly impassable roads to minister to this family.

"Who will care for this outcast Russian family if we don't?" they ask. "These are *'naschi,'* one of our own Russian people."

And *naschi* continue to enroll in the only Russian Bible Institute in the world. It's the school that prayer built, and the school that functions today by the same spiritual discipline.

11

Fruit in New Orchards

The misery of World War II lingered on in the wretched European camps designed for displaced persons spun off from the horror of the conflict. These crowded caldrons of human misery became homes for thousands of Slavic refugees who had been thrust out of their countries or who refused to return to Russia after the war. Year after year they waited in congested camps in Germany and Austria, hoping for resettlement and a new life in a free country. Among the two million "DPs," often treated as non-persons, were souls for whom Christ died. Peter Deyneka launched a gospel offensive to reach them.

The Slavic Gospel Association headquarters became a depot for processing hundreds of food and clothing packages to Slavic displaced persons. With the relief parcels went missionaries to offer the Bread of Life as well.

For the rest of the decade of the '40s and into the '50s Peter traveled continually to the camps in many parts of Europe. Sometimes he would remain there several months. Hearts were opened to receive the Good Seed. Young Slavic workers from North America joined Peter for the twin thrusts of relief and evangelism to a captive mission field ripe for Kingdom harvests.

The recruitment of young evangelists for the camps was an effective strategy for drawing into the mission many lifetime missionaries. What the young people saw they could never forget. The meetings generated a new compassion for their own people and fired their zeal to be Christ's hands and feet and ears and voice among them.

One of the first recruits was Ruth Deyneka, eldest daughter of Peter and Vera. After graduating from Bob Jones University, Ruth accompanied her father to Europe to work in the refugee camps for the summer. But at the end of the ninety-day stint Ruth didn't want to leave. Her heart had been broken by the desperate needs of the DPs.

On the day she was to sail home with her father she made her decision to remain. She went to Southampton, England, with her father and helped him unpack in his stateroom aboard the *Queen Mary* that would carry him to the United States.

"Are you sure you want to stay in Europe, Ruthie?" Peter asked.

"Yes, papa, I'm sure"

"Do you need some money?"

Ruth shook her head. "Why do I need money? I have ten dollars in my pocketbook, friends back in the United States who care about my ministry, and my ticket to get back to the refugee camp in Germany. If mama sends me CARE packages I'll be all right."

Peter wept as he hugged his daughter and said good-bye. They knelt together and prayed, committing each other to the Lord. "Her courage touched my heart," he said later.

Back in the DP camps Ruth was joined by Roza Kucher, a girl of Russian heritage from a Slavic community in Western Canada. For a year and a half they ministered together, sang hymns, and played their instruments.

Roza vividly recalls one incident when she and Ruth were conducting a meeting in a German camp.

"I stood on the platform—one young, rather tremulous girl, facing rows of haggard, sad, Slavic people," Roza said. "I had just finished speaking from the Bible and praying. I asked all who wanted to accept Christ as Savior to stand. In response, the entire audience rose. I began to weep at the evident heart hunger, feeling helpless to counsel so many. I had studied personal evangelism as a student in the Toronto Russian Bible Institute, but I never expected anything like this.

"My co-laborer, Ruth, was also choked with emotion. 'Pray, Roz,' she whispered, 'Pray! Tell the people to repeat the prayer after you.'

"As I prayed each phrase a roar of response resounded from the audience. Hearts were eagerly opened to receive the Lord."

The fruit was ripe. Happy were the reapers to whom God gave the harvest!

Both Roza and Ruth met their future husbands in Europe. In 1951 Nick Leonovich, a Russian relative of the Deynekas from New Jersey, felt God's call to work among the displaced persons. In Europe he met and married Roza, where they continued their ministries under the sponsorship of the Slavic Gospel Association.

In 1958 Nick and Roza initiated gospel broadcasts in Russian at Trans World Radio which Paul Freed founded in Tangier, Morocco. Later Nick and Roza continued this radio ministry to Russian-speaking people from Monte Carlo, Monaco.

Earlier Peter Deyneka had met with Dr. Paul Freed and his father Ralph of Trans World Radio. The three men met in Times Square Hotel in New York City. They discussed the possibility of Russian broadcasts from the proposed radio station in Tangier. Peter Deyneka suggested Nick

Leonovich as the Russian radio speaker for the new station. The three men prayed together and committed this to the Lord, never dreaming of the tremendous future outreach the station in Tangier, and later the ones in Monaco and Bonaire, would have in future years. Over the years gospel broadcasts beamed from the TWR transmitters have brought bounteous blessings to the Soviet Union.

In a DP camp at Trieste, Italy, Ruth met Jack Shalanko who had also graduated from the Toronto Russian Bible Institute. They were married in Chicago by Ruth's father, after which they also continued their global ministries at a shortwave radio microphone—theirs being at Radio Station HCJB, Quito, Ecuador.

From among the ranks of the DPs missionaries emerged. Agripina Bardanova had been a wealthy woman in Russia before the great war. In the early 1900s she made a profitable living smuggling saccharin from Siberia to Western Russia. In 1929 she married and moved with her husband to Latvia.

As the bride of a successful businessman she had all the material comforts and the social prestige anyone could want. She had three homes and money to travel, yet to her dismay she was unhappy—restless and searching.

In 1929 Agripina heard Oswald J. Smith of Toronto, Canada, when he visited Riga, Latvia. She opened her heart in that service and experienced the transforming power of Jesus Christ. She began at once to witness of her faith to others. As she had conducted the other affairs of her business life she worked equally as fervently for her new Master.

Ten years later World War II drove Agripina and her husband to Italy. There her husband died. Agripina was left penniless. Missionaries of the Slavic Gospel Association found her in Rome and assisted Agripina in her dire poverty. The widow heard Peter Deyneka preach and determined she would spend the rest of her life witnessing among her own people. Today she is elderly but still energetically carrying out a witness among Slavic immigrants and Italians in Rome.

The Slavic Gospel Association supplied and delivered thousands of relief packages to displaced persons and refugees in Europe after World War II.

Peter with a large refugee family holding their rations for the week, in front of their barracks in Austria. This picture was taken soon after World War II.

There was a tearful farewell when daughter Ruth (seated second from left) decided to remain in Europe to minister to the refugees.

Peter with Bob Evans (standing, center) in Poland with Christian youth leaders immediately after World War II. Bob Evans later founded the Greater European Mission.

With Russian refugees in Rome, Italy, who today are reaching newly arrived Russian Jews from the U.S.S.R.

She has distributed tens of thousands of gospel tracts and declares, "I will never retire from serving Christ. I'll only stop when the Lord takes me home."

In 1951, during one of many trips to DP camps, Peter Deyneka was accompanied by his son, Peter, Jr., a second-year student at Wheaton College.

The young man had been trained for such excursions from his boyhood by his godly parents who had faithfully prepared their children to serve Christ. Despite protests that "we are American now, Papa," all three children had lessons in the Russian language so they would be better equipped to minister to Slavic people. Young Peter often accompanied his father to meetings where he played his trombone or the piano. After graduating from Wheaton College, Peter, Jr. attended Northern Baptist Seminary in Chicago where he earned a Master of Divinity Degree. Afterward he was commissioned to several mission fields: two years in Alaska, one in Ecuador, two as a teacher at the Russian Bible School in Argentina, one in Europe, and a year and a half as a radio missionary at Radio Station HLKX, in South Korea. Peter, Jr. has visited Russia three times and in 1975, when his father retired as General Director, Peter, Jr. was appointed by the Executive Committee of the Slavic Gospel Association to take his father's place.

During the years that Peter Deyneka was circling the globe, establishing new missionary outreaches and ministering to Russians, he also tirelessly cultivated supporters in North America. Hardly an evangelical Christian was without some knowledge of the man who was "rushing the gospel to the Russians."

During his years at Wheaton College, Peter Deyneka, Jr. participated in a gospel team which traveled each weekend to churches throughout the Midwest and as far south as Florida. At each church people would approach Peter and say, "I know your father." This happened so frequently that the leader of the team, Leighton Ford, began to introduce

Peter, Jr. as "Peter I-know-your-father Deyneka." The son recalls in two years of such travel only two churches where his father had not previously visited.

The senior Peter Deyneka's "home" for a good portion of the time was a hotel room or a train depot or an airport. "I felt like I knew the inside of every train and plane," he said. "Sometimes the stations seemed like my home."

Peter's broken English and short-clipped syntax, laced with a heavy Russian accent, could have impeded his presentation. But he turned it to his advantage and through his thundering sermons and strong missionary appeals earned well the nickname "Peter Dynamite." People who heard his powerful messages often commented, "He carries his own loudspeaker with him wherever he goes."

From big churches (such as Peoples Church of Toronto where he often shared the pulpit with Pastor Oswald J. Smith) to tiny churches he went, calling for helpers to give the gospel to Slavic peoples.

One of the smaller congregations was the Farmerstown Mennonite Church in Ohio with a tiny missionary budget. Pastor Homer Kandel had become concerned about the church's ignorance of missions. The book *Much Prayer, Much Power* fell into his hands, and later its author came to speak. Peter's book, along with volumes by Oswald J. Smith, greatly influenced Homer Kandel and his people to become active in missions.

The first year, with eighty members, the Farmerstown Mennonites pledged the astonishing (for a church of their size) amount of eight thousand dollars. People later wept when the pledges added up to more than sixteen thousand dollars the first Sunday of a missionary conference at the end of the year. The second year the offerings increased to twenty-five thousand dollars; the third year to thirty-five thousand dollars and in the fourth year, with a church membership increase of only twelve people, the pledge figure was forty-five thousand dollars. To date, the latest pledge is a yearly one hundred thousand dollars plus. And the fervor has spread to other churches.

Slavic Gospel Association, in the early 1940s, had opened branch offices in England, Australia, New Zealand, and South America to serve believers outside North America whose hearts God had touched by appeals to help.

The list of men supporting Peter's ministry grew larger with the spread of the mission's scope: Torrey Johnson, Roy Strobeck, Bob Swanson, Robert Kinney, Eugene Johnson, Warren Wiersbe, Charles Bodeen, Evon Hedley, Bob Cook, Jack Wyrtzen, Billy Graham, the late Charles E. Fuller, George Sweeting, Robert Bowman, Stephen Olford, and many others.

In an amazing fashion Peter, unlettered in the deeper tenets of theology and unlearned in school-taught methods of evangelism, nearly always enjoyed spiritual power in his sermons and fruit for his labors. His message was simple and powerful. So were his tastes for material blessings. A loaf of black bread and a tube of salami from his brief case were enough to set out a meal to relish.

Once in Liverpool, England, following World War II, he went with Billy Graham and Cliff and Billie Barrows to a restaurant. Billy Graham was conducting evangelistic services in the Liverpool City auditorium. Peter Deyneka was speaking at SGA meetings in England. The two men had met and prayed together for God's blessings as they preached in England.

In the wake of the war, rations at the restaurant were scarce. Very little bread was available. Peter pulled a tube of salami and dark bread carefully wrapped in newspaper from his ubiquitous suitcase. Billie Barrows had some butter from a rationing coupon, so bread was distributed and meat provided to the grateful participants in the humble meal.

In mass meetings or to individuals, Peter was ready in

season and out to talk about his Lord. On a trip to Australia in the 1960s he had to wait four hours for a changeover flight. A stewardess asked Peter, "And what business are you in?"

"I'm a preacher of the gospel," Peter replied.

"What is the gospel?" asked the puzzled stewardess.

The girl had only a few minutes left to visit. Quickly Peter showed her from the Bible the hope of the gospel for all people.

"That's strange," the girl replied. "I've been in church for seventeen years and I've never even heard the word 'gospel' in our church." She asked several more questions, then turned to leave.

"Would you like to know Christ as your personal Savior?" Peter asked.

"Yes," the stewardess replied softly.

Peter prayed with her and promised to send her a New Testament and his book, *Much Prayer, Much Power*.

Several weeks later Peter was passing through Sydney again en route to the Philippine Islands when the same stewardess approached him. "Do you remember me?" she asked, smiling. "I received your literature and read half of your book. I'm going to read the rest, too. I'm following the Lord now."

In hometown Chicago, Peter's "Jerusalem," for forty-five years the Slavic Gospel Association sponsored Russian meetings in various parts of the city. SGA also sponsors a weekly gospel radio broadcast in Russian from a Chicago station.

Basil, a Russian emigrant to Chicago, was a drug addict. He came to the Russian meeting of the SGA in Chicago, spoke of his addiction to drugs, and expressed his opinion that his case was hopeless. Peter urged him not to give up. "Please keep coming to our meetings," he advised. "You will hear the gospel and I am praying for you."

The desperate boy was so lonely to hear Russian spoken

that he returned again and again. Each time the message of the gospel penetrated deeper.

He was eventually converted and afterward attended Bible school—another trophy of grace, the outcome of persistence and faithful witnessing. Today he is a pastor in the eastern United States. In more than half a century of preaching, the number of "Basils" influenced by Peter Deyneka are vast and without number.

Once a bashful peasant boy in Russia by the Wisla River—now a bold proclaimer of the gospel, crossing many oceans and all continents on errands for the King of kings. Because one lonely immigrant from the Old World found new life at Moody Church in Chicago, many thousands will enjoy the eternal bliss of heaven.

12

No Roof over Russia

At the flash of the red light "ON THE AIR" Peter leaned forward in his chair and began: "Dorogeeye Radioslushatelyee."

In less than a second those words were flung across the ocean from Quito, Ecuador, to Chomsk . . . Kiev . . . Moscow . . . and the plains of Siberia. The date was 1941. The new tool of evangelism by radio among Slavic people had begun its strategic endeavor.

Other mission agencies would eventually follow the pioneer, until as many as a thousand gospel broadcasts in Russian each month would flood Peter's native land, beamed from the crackling transmitters of ten international radio stations.

The six hundred broadcasts beamed toward Russia each month by the Slavic Gospel Association reach more people than the apostle Paul addressed throughout his lifetime.

The message with which Peter Deyneka initiated gospel broadcasts for Slavic people was picked up in Chicago by his wife on a shortwave receiver. She sent a cable which read: "Glad to hear your voice and message—came very clear."

Peter delivered sixteen daily broadcasts in Russian over Radio Station HCJB, then hurried home to Chicago to enlist radio preachers to continue the effort. His first recruit was Chicagoan Constantine Lewshenia, a graduate of Moody Bible Institute, who later led the pioneering project to build the permanent Russian Bible Institute in Argentina, along with Slavic Gospel Association missionaries Sam and Mary Fewchuk and Andrew Prokopchuk.

Alex Leonovich, a young missionary evangelist, later joined the Russian-language staff of Radio Station HCJB and had the joy of learning that he had led his own brother Nick, six thousand miles away in New Jersey, to a deeper commitment to Christ by radio. Seventeen-year-old Nick bowed his head at the shortwave receiver that day, and God changed the course of his life by sending him into missionary radio work to reach the people in Russia, from whence his parents had brought him as an infant, as a missionary.

Peter Deyneka watched closely the response to his original sixteen radio sermons from HCJB. He quickly became convinced that this vast and fruitful medium for the gospel could be utilized successfully to reach beyond the "Iron Curtain."

Bibles, seemingly the most significant way to feed spiritually hungry Slavs, were frequently allowed no farther than the Soviet border. Despite all the creative and persistent ways that were tried to carry Bibles beyond the border, the trickle getting through did not begin to meet the demands of 250 million people in the Soviet Union. But the long arm of radio could reach the ears of eager listeners. This miracle offered unparalleled opportunities to share the gospel of the Lord Jesus Christ with the millions in atheistic countries. Some forty million shortwave radio receivers are in use in the USSR.

Because their own internal stations utilize shortwave, Russians traditionally invest heavily in these radio receivers. The shortwave radios are large and powerful enough to receive broadcasts from Christian stations in

148

Alaska, Korea, Western Europe, the Philippines, United States, and South America. Many listeners write to say the radio programs are their only church. Peter and his staff know that their unseen congregation is a large one.

A Siberian listener shared this burst of enthusiasm for radio evangelism: "If you were to preach to a crowd of ten thousand, that would only be ten thousand. But when you preach over the radio, hundreds of thousands—even millions!—listen to you. Many are buying radios for the first time for the sole purpose of listening to you. Those who do not have enough money pool their funds with others to buy a radio. When you pray, we pray. Thousands of people all across the USSR are joining you in prayer."

Listeners have requested broadcasters to "read the Scriptures on your radio programs, but please don't read so fast. We cannot keep up writing!" Since radio is often the main source of Christian information for Russian believers, missionaries prepare special programs to instruct lay preachers in addition to reading the Bible at dictation speed so that listeners can write down portions of the Holy Writ into notebooks and have part of the Bible for their very own. Other specialized programs are broadcast for Russian children who have no Sunday schools. Such schools and all Christian youth activities are illegal in the USSR.

In addition, the Slavic Gospel Association conducts a "Bible Institute of the Air" for Soviet listeners. The program features daily Bible studies and exposition of the Scriptures, systematically progressing through the Bible for the benefit of lay preachers and church leaders who depend upon this grist for their weekly sermons. There are no Bible schools or seminaries for evangelical Christians anywhere in Russia.

From the Ukraine came this letter:

"If it is possible, send us at least two or three of your songs so that when you sing these hymns, we can join in your beautiful singing. . . . We don't have a Bible and we don't

149

At the invitation of Dr. Clarence Jones, the first Gospel broadcasts were beamed into the U.S.S.R. in Russian by Peter Deyneka over the pioneer missionary radio station HCJB.

Mr. and Mrs. Deyneka with the Russian Department staff at HCJB in Quito, Ecuador, where their daughter and son-in-law Jack Shalanko have ministered for many years.

Russian radio staff in Chicago headquarters preparing some of the six hundred Gospel programs beamed into Russia monthly.

"Bread from heaven" arriving in Russian over the air-waves to eager listeners. Many preachers depend on the broadcasts for their Bible study.

have fellowship with other Christians because there are no Christians nearby. All we can do is pray and continue to listen to your programs."

In Kuybishev, Russia, a listener wrote: "I am twenty-three years old and have completed nine years of education. I work in a factory as a lathe operator. I spend most of my spare time by the radio listening to musical programs on foreign stations. This is how I accidentally came across your programs. Personally, I don't consider myself a believer or an unbeliever. I've never attended any religious gathering in this city, and don't even know if any exist. But no matter what anyone says, I am interested in listening to your programs."

A student wrote from Siberia, a land area larger than the United States, where fifty million people live: "I have been listening to your broadcasts regularly for four years now. Here in Siberia, in the town of M_____ as well as in other towns, there are many Christians and others listening to your programs."

Dimitri Alexeyevich was twenty-three and in love. But the girl he wanted to marry spurned his proposal. Enraged, Dimitri tried to kill his sweetheart. She recovered, but the young man was sentenced to ten years in a Russian prison.

Slavic Gospel Association missionary Nick Leonovich, head of the Russian Department at Trans World Radio station in Monte Carlo, received this letter from Dimitri: "I came across your Christian programs on my transistor radio here at the prison farm, and they made a positive impression upon my miserable soul. Now I cannot live even one day without listening to your spiritual broadcasts. But can the Lord forgive a sin so great as mine? I want to follow Christ. . . ."

Radio provided an opening wedge for Slavic missionaries who traveled in Eastern Europe.

Pastor L. took the train to meet citizens of a small village in the north country of Poland who were regular listeners to Polish gospel programs. He planned on his first visit just to meet the six listeners who had written to request Bibles.

But by the time he arrived at the fourth house, such a large group of children were following him that he sat down and began telling them stories from the Bible. He also taught them to sing gospel hymns.

Suddenly a young Polish man excitedly rushed up to him and announced, "Sir, you must come to my house now and have a meeting. We are all waiting for you. Believers from all over the village have come together to hear you preach."

As Pastor L. approached the house he was amazed to see it jammed with people. Some were standing outside the door; others were looking in through the windows.

At one end of the parlor he noticed a statue of Mary and two candles displayed on a table. He had anticipated a Protestant meeting, forgetting that most of the people in the countryside were Roman Catholic.

"May the name of Jesus Christ be blessed," Pastor L. exclaimed as he entered the room.

All the people responded: "And forever and ever may it be blessed."

Villagers, who had not been encouraged by their church to read the Bible, were noticeably excited when their visiting speaker opened his copy of the Word of God and began to speak. No one moved for an hour as he expounded unto them more perfectly the grace of God and the love of the Savior for the lost.

When he had finished speaking, Pastor L. suggested he teach them a song about God's love. As if they were children, they eagerly memorized each phrase.

For three hours the villagers remained squeezed into the small room, singing and listening as Pastor L. talked to them about the Lord. Fearful that such a meeting might arouse antagonism on the part of the authorities, he told them he must leave.

"I have copies of God's Book here if you want one for yourself," he said holding a New Testament above his head.

The people pressed forward to receive a copy.

"Wait!" a farmer exclaimed. He took his hat, shook it out and passed it around. "Let us show our gratitude by helping to pay for the Bibles," he said.

Finally the crowd moved away. One old man remained behind. "I must show you something," he told Pastor L.

He brought out a large, old Polish New Testament—so old that many pages were soiled and crumbling.

"My father was in the Russian navy during the Russo-Japanese War of 1905 in Korea," he said. "There an American missionary gave him this Bible. When my father died, he left it to me. All these years I have waited for someone to come and explain this book."

The hunger of these villagers for spiritual food is typical of millions in areas served by broadcasts in Slavic languages. Excerpts from the steady flow of letters sent by listeners reveal hearts that are seeking to make peace with the Creator.

On an open post card from the Ukraine: "What a joy it is to listen to your broadcasts! There is no greater thrill for me than to have fellowship with His children. I am so thankful to God for the opportunity of hearing His tender voice through your lips."

From Kazakhstan, USSR: "When you are on the air, you ask us to let you hear from us; we would answer immediately if we could. . . . One Sunday recently, after the morning meeting, a dear sister in the Lord told me the following about her husband who is now dead.

"This couple listened frequently to HCJB and Jack Shalanko's messages always gripped him. As a result he accepted the Lord. Then he became ill and passed through great suffering in the hospital. As his wife sat beside his bed he lifted his hand. She asked what he wanted. 'I want to hear Brother Shalanko preach,' he murmured. They tried to tune in the radio. Shortly after that he was taken home. Just before he died, his wife asked him, 'What heritage are you leaving us?' He answered with the words of a hymn,

155

'Christ's precious blood and righteousness, which is my jewel and my attire.' "

Not every writer is sympathetic to the gospel messages preached on the broadcasts. A listener from Kirkhiz, USSR, wrote: "I often listen to your broadcasts and for a long time have wanted to talk with you, but do not know if this will work out. However, I decided to try.

"Your broadcast, of course, is not dangerous; you do not touch politics; and for the most part I like your singing and music. I always enjoy music, regardless of who transmits it, and even though I may not understand the words, nevertheless, music always has a pleasing effect on me.

"But this is not the whole matter. You in your broadcast really do convincingly ask listeners to pray to God and ask Him for mercy that He would forgive us our sins. About what kind of sins are you speaking? Can it really be that we have so many of them that we should ask for mercy and, as you say, a miracle will happen?

"Even here in the USSR, fifty years ago people believed this nonsense; nevertheless God didn't help them very well.

"The question that is of great interest to me is this: You friends believe in a god? Do you believe sincerely or because of your wages? Very likely you do not live by miracles but by some kind of means.

"There has not been such a miracle that a man living in a thatched-roofed hut woke up in the morning to find himself in a new metal-roofed house with an orchard around it and birds-of-paradise singing outside. Or, for instance, one does not have money, but prays earnestly, and there is a miracle! If God existed and there were such miracles, people would not fight but live in harmony; they would just have to spend a night in earnest prayer and all would be well. But God is very friendly with the wealthy and powerful.

"Do not be offended with me, dear friends. You ask us to write, so read this, and if it is not too much bother, write me an answer. I shall be very glad to receive it. May your letter

156

to me be a miracle. I send you my best wishes and Christmas greetings.''

Everywhere Peter Deyneka traveled he found fruit from the "miracle electronic missionary." While speaking at an evangelistic meeting in Argentina one time, Peter was introduced to a young man who had come to sing and play the accordion.

Before the man began, he turned to Peter and said, "Mr. Deyneka, you and the people in this meeting don't realize this, but you are my spiritual father. In 1950, I became a Christian through your ministry. I remember well the night when you spoke and I gave my heart to Christ. That night my life was changed.

"In 1957, after I was converted, my parents decided to return to Russia from Argentina. I returned with them, but this was a time of great struggle in my life. I was full of turmoil and sadness.

"Through much prayer I finally realized that being in Russia was God's will for me and I submitted my life to Christ and tried to serve Him there.

"I remember when I arrived with my parents in a Russian village in 1957. At that time, the people were not acquainted with the gospel broadcasts from Ecuador. I introduced them to these regular programs

"One man had just sold his radio because he was tired of listening to propaganda programs. But as soon as he learned about your broadcasts he bought another radio and started listening to the gospel broadcasts from HCJB. 'Why didn't you come to Russia sooner so you could have told me about these wonderful programs?' he asked. 'Then I would have kept my first radio. But it was worth it to buy another one!'

"Shortly after our arrival, many other Christians began listening to the radio broadcasts. I know for a fact that hundreds of thousands of people in the Soviet Union are listening to the Russian broadcasts of the Slavic Gospel Association. I know, because I lived among these people.''

Thus the long arms of radio embrace the globe. Many will be in heaven because Peter Deyneka launched a new medium for the gospel to Russians a quarter of a century ago, proving again his obedience to preach the gospel "by all means" everywhere.

Not all of the several thousand letter replies mailed to listeners each year by SGA missionaries reach the eager correspondents. Censorship is alive and active against such letters. But all letters are answered just the same, believer to believer, reaching out in Christian love within the vast fellowship that knows no international barriers.

13

A Famine of Bread

During the mid-1920s the USSR authorized a major printing of Bibles in the Russian language. There has been little since.

An approximate total of fifty thousand Bibles was printed in the Soviet Union for evangelicals with official sanction in the years of 1957, 1968, and 1974. But these token printings were not enough to satisfy the spiritual thirst of Russia's millions.

When the Slavic Gospel Association was founded, the demand for Bibles and gospel literature in Russia had already become desperate. Peter Deyneka was rarely out of earshot of his brethren's pleas for God's Word in print. Thus he decided "printed missionaries must be part of the SGA program."

Literature, after all, never grew weary, never argued, complained, or needed support. It adapted itself to the culture of a province and spoke even when discarded.

Gradually, shelves at SGA headquarters began filling up with stockpiles of Russian literature earmarked for the

USSR and beyond, where it was used in soul-winning expeditions and for Bible teaching conferences.

The Soviet Union, a society officially atheistic, fears the Bible. The official Soviet encyclopedia states that the Bible is a compilation of Jewish myths . . . that Jesus was a mythological character. "No such person ever existed," the encyclopedia declares. This volume is the official reference work used by Russia's 250 million people. Many wish they could know the truth about Jesus Christ.

To counter the natural inclination of many spiritually hungry Russian people toward faith and godliness, the Soviet atheists print more books annually than any other country in the world. Included is a vast proliferation of atheistic material of various types.

In one year, the Soviet Union published 284 book titles and hundreds of thousands of copies on the subject of atheism. In addition, articles on the virtues of atheism were placed in periodicals whose circulations ran into the multimillions. The output of religious literature, by contrast, was almost zero.

But the fruitless promises of atheism do not satisfy those who have learned the truth of God. Their search for the Word of Life goes on.

A missionary sponsored by the Slavic Gospel Association traveling as a tourist recently took several Bibles and Christian books into Siberia. In one large church he gave the pastor a Bible and also a copy of *The Life of Jesus Christ*, a Russian pictorial book of the Gospels for young people.

The pastor held the pictorial book in his hand and gently, lovingly turned the colorful pages with a smile on his face. "This is for children?" he questioned. "Why, even our adults have never seen anything so beautiful as this book!"

Other brethren spotted the pastor with the book and began pressing in close for a look. "We want it next!" they exclaimed.

A Siberian Christian with a crippled arm traveled over five thousand miles to Moscow to find a Bible. He returned rejoicing with his treasure.

The fervent prayers of Russian Christians praying for the "Bread of Life" impressed and burdened Peter Deyneka deeply.

Peter Deyneka reported that large congregations of Russian believers came to church an hour before the service just to hear the Bible being read.

Packages of Bibles, hymn books, and Christian literature being shipped out by SGA workers to give Slavic people the "Bread of Life."

Peter noticed that the splendid Russian choirs and the congregations often sang either from memory or from hand-written hymn books.

"You'll have to form a line," the pastor directed, "and sign a list so everyone can share alike."

The line snaked down the aisle and around the outside wall as Christians, eager for devotional material to read, patiently waited their turn for a few precious days to share the book.

With tears, the pastor thanked the visitor that day for the "children's" book. "Two books for five hundred people," he sighed. "Could you somehow bring us more?"

When Christians in the Soviet Union hear about friends from the West coming to visit them with Christian literature, they sometimes fast and pray for one month for the safe arrival of both the messenger and the printed material.

During one of his recent trips to the USSR, Peter Deyneka noticed a man following him as he left the church where he had just preached.

"Brother Deyneka!" the man called. "I plead with you in the name of the Lord, give me your New Testament."

Peter stopped and looked at the stranger sorrowfully. "I'm sorry," he said. "I have no more because I have given them all away."

The man shook his head. "Surely you have one more—your own copy perhaps? I had so longed and hoped for the Bread of Life. . . ."

Peter laid a hand on the man's shoulder. "I'm so sorry," he repeated. "I do not have a single copy left."

The man went away sad, typical of thousands who longed to be spiritually nourished by the Bread of Life.

Appeals for Bibles to the Slavic Gospel Association have never stopped. From each trip to Europe Peter and his co-workers returned with stories of people who were prepared to sacrifice as much as a month's wages to obtain the precious volume of sacred writings.

One Christian man in Russia finally received a Bible after waiting many years. He opened the cover and began to read: "The New Testament of our Lord Jesus Christ." Tears came to his eyes and he said, "This is the most important book in the world. The message of this book will give me new courage."

Another person in the Soviet Union declared, "I am ready to be without anything . . . but not without the Word of God."

In the Ukraine, so many people signed up to have a copy of the Bible for one week that the pastor estimated it would take seven months to serve all who had expressed a wish to take their turn in reading it.

One day in Moscow, a Christian brother who had heard him speak approached Peter hesitantly. "Brother Deyneka," he began, "when you finish visiting Russia, what are you going to do with your New Testament?"

"Well, I always carry a New Testament with me . . ."

"Brother Deyneka, there is a preacher in Leningrad who has no New Testament. How wonderful it would be if you could give him yours as a gift."

When Peter arrived in Leningrad to visit the church he approached the first man he saw inside. "I am looking for Brother Vasiliy," he said.

"I am he," the Russian replied.

Peter pulled out his New Testament. "Then this is yours as a gift. But I apologize that the cover is worn."

The Russian was seized with deep emotion as he eagerly accepted the gift. "Oh, Brother Deyneka, we are not looking for beautiful covers. We are looking for the Word of God!" he exclaimed.

The man gently laid his treasure on his desk. Then he tenderly lifted it up and looked at it again. Then he shook Peter's hand enthusiastically in gratitude for the means to improve his preaching of the truth of God.

God uses unusual means to open up ways to allow this gospel literature to be taken in by workers of the Slavic Gospel Association and their friends in Europe.

Two men—a Siberian Christian and an SGA

missionary—stood in the bitter, wintry cold one morning in Moscow. The Siberian, with a handless arm hanging limply at his side, told the missionary tourist that he had traveled some five thousand miles with one purpose—to find and take back a Bible so he could "teach God's Word" to his small congregation of believers.

In Moscow he providentially met this visiting missionary from the Slavic Gospel Association who could supply the treasure he sought. The missionary had one Bible left in his hotel room. Seeing the man's faith, he felt compelled to surrender his last Bible to this crippled lay preacher who had traveled so far in search of God's Word.

While the missionary tourist went to his room to get the Bible the Siberian preacher waited in the lobby. When the Bible came, the excited preacher embraced the missionary with his good arm and exclaimed loudly in the carefully watched lobby, "God be praised!"

Then to the consternation of the visitor and to the amazement of the Soviet hotel management, the old minister fearlessly dropped to his knees. Without concern for his own safety he cried, "Let us pray right here! I must thank the Lord now for this great gift."

Afterward he prepared to leave. "I am going straight to the train station and back to Siberia," he said. "I have found what I came for."

How do Russian Christians get God's Word for themselves in the Soviet Union? A great number of Bibles come into the communist world through tourists as has just been described. Christians also treasure the old Bibles which were printed many years ago. These are bound and rebound and protected as rare treasures of vintage.

The majority of Christians, however, must resort to the same methods as people did before the printing press was invented. That is, they copy God's Word into a notebook. Christians attempt to borrow a Bible from somewhere for a few days in order to copy as much as possible into their notebook. Or else they will listen to radio broadcasts from outside and copy down the Scripture into their notebook. Some Christians have copied the entire Bible into notebook form.

Sometimes when Christians gain possession of a complete Bible they divide it up into book sections so that thirty or forty of their friends will at least have part of the Bible, rather than one person keeping the entire Bible for himself. It is continually circulating. If a borrower keeps a copy too long he will be reminded that others are waiting to use it.

Whenever Peter visited Russia, believers would beg for Bibles, pleading with him quietly but earnestly for the Word of God. Many showed him borrowed "Bibles" copied by hand. Many had to take their turn reading copies lent to them by their pastor.

On one of his trips to Russia, Peter Deyneka, Jr., on a cold, windy day noticed two women with flimsy top coats in a park near a church in which he was to speak. One was reading aloud while the other listened. Both ignored the bitter weather.

Quietly a third joined them on the park bench, then a fourth and a fifth. Finally there were six women huddled on the bench listening to the reading from the volume which was evidently precious. He soon realized that the women were Christian believers, and that their treasure was a copy of God's Word which the owner was sharing in the park.

In a Christian home, Peter, Jr. gave the children of the family a copy of the *Life of Jesus Christ*. Immediately the children scampered away with the book. Later Peter heard them crying. He learned that they all wanted to read the book at the same time. They had never seen such a Christian book for youth before.

One of the most saddening experiences in life is to meet a Christian who begs for a Bible or some other piece of literature and not to have it to give to him.

Peter Deyneka, Jr. also met a young man in his twenties after a service in northern Russia. The young man asked Peter if by any chance he might have a Russian Bible that he could give him. Peter, with great regret, told him that he did not. The ones he had brought had already been distributed. Then the young Russian Christian told Peter a story. He lived in the city of Novosibirsk in central Siberia more than three thousand miles from the city in which he was now standing. He was on his vacation. He was spending his entire vacation traveling thousands of miles and spending a lot of money for the sole purpose of finding a Bible for himself.

The young believer turned away sadly. He had come with high hope; he now left dejectedly, realizing that he might actually have to return home empty-handed.

There are believers in the USSR today who have waited all their adult lives for a copy of God's Word, and still their hands are empty. It is impossible to buy a Bible or a Christian book in any book store in the Soviet Union.

"Please," comes the familiar cry, "bring us the Bread of Life."

14

Much Prayer, Much Power!

Peter Deyneka was never afraid to pray—not afraid to lose sleep and appeal to God in "strong crying and tears" for the needs of his growing mission. And, in return, amazing things happened. The heavenly answers were no surprise to Peter. He knew God was listening. The Creator's arm was not shortened.

"Little prayer, little power," Peter often admonished his friends, "but much prayer, much power!"

At the start of his Christian life, Peter learned the power of prayer at Cedar Lake Bible Conference in Indiana, founded by Paul Rader in the early twenties. Paul Rader would announce special prayer meetings for men in a woods near the camp. He often asked Peter to lead those meetings. Later, in 1930, when Rader was conducting Bible conferences at Lake Harbor, Michigan (now Maranatha Bible Conference), Peter was put in charge of the sessions in a Prayer Tower overlooking the grounds and Lake Michigan. Peter's enthusiasm for prayer led many conferees to that tower where lives were transformed and where thousands of dollars were raised for the work of the Lord.

On August 9, 1925, after spending a night in prayer, Peter was able to say Yes to God and make plans to return as a missionary to his native land. Although he had no resources at the time, he thanked God for supplying his needs, and before long his ticket and money for expenses were supplied.

In the early years of the Youth for Christ movement following World War II, Peter's contribution to the team efforts were super doses of prayer—all-night sessions which brought heaven close and unleashed spiritual power.

A Youth for Christ rally was scheduled in Chicago's vast Soldier Field on a Memorial Day weekend. For three weeks before the rally it had rained steadily every day, threatening to cancel the rally. Much preparation had been made and much money spent for advertising. YFC President Torrey Johnson phoned Peter an SOS.

"We must have a twenty-four-hour prayer meeting, Peter," he said. "And I want you to lead it."

Christian leaders, pastors, and laymen gathered at the Sherman Hotel in downtown Chicago to ask God to stop the rain so the meeting could be held.

"As we prayed for it to stop, we could hear the rain falling outside," Peter recalls. "It was difficult for some to keep going."

Two hours before the twenty-four-hour prayer vigil was scheduled to end, Peter stopped the meeting. "We have been praying for the rain to stop," he reminded the gathered intercessors. "Now let us spend the next two hours thanking God that there will be no rain tomorrow!"

The next morning the rain had vanished. Sunshine bathed the rain-soaked city, although for five miles all around Chicago the rain kept falling.

More than sixty-five thousand people gathered at Soldier Field to hear the singing, testimonies, and gospel message. Hundreds of people committed their lives to the Lord Jesus Christ.

The service closed; the people went home rejoicing and praising God. And the next day the long siege of rain started again, and it continued to rain for several days afterward.

Through the ministry of Youth for Christ, and particularly through the dynamic Youth for Christ prayer meetings at the summer YFC conferences at Winona Lake, Peter Deyneka became well-acquainted with the young evangelist Billy Graham, whom he had first met while Graham was a student at Trinity Bible College in Florida.

In 1949, in Los Angeles, Evangelist Billy Graham held his first major city-wide crusade. Graham invited Peter Deyneka to come to Los Angeles before the crusade to spend a few days praying together and seeking God for His blessing on the meetings. Billy Graham was very conscious of the fact that without the blessing and power of God upon his ministry, there would be little eternal value accomplished. Their prayers were heard. Many came to Christ.

One summer in Europe, where Peter was speaking on the victorious spiritual life, a woman came to him weeping following one of his messages. "My husband is an unbeliever," she said. "I have lost patience with him."

Peter challenged her: "Stop preaching at him and start praying for him and live a Christian life before him."

Three months later he learned that God had saved her husband in answer to the wife's steady, faithful prayer. The man finally came to a service with his wife and put his trust in Christ.

In the first letter Peter received from his home in Russia in five years, his father wrote in 1922 that the family was dying from starvation. Three of Peter's brothers and two sisters had already perished because of the scourge of famine which swept the nation following World War I.

Peter spent a day and a night in prayer for his parents and one brother, Andrei, who were left alive. His appetite left him. In desperation he would not give up praying until he felt assured that God would answer and help his family.

The morning after his all-night prayer vigil, a Christian friend came to see him.

"I have not been able to sleep because of a burden," she

admitted. "Do you have someone in Russia that you could send money to to help buy food?"

Peter asked how she knew about the terrible suffering his parents were going through.

"God laid it on my heart and I felt there must be a need," she said.

"Praise the Lord!" Peter exclaimed. He dispatched the money immediately so his family could buy food.

During his first visit to his parents' home in Russia after traveling to America and finding the Lord, his mother admitted she "had religion," but did not know Christ as her personal Lord and Savior. Because of this, Peter met intense opposition to his message.

For nearly a year he endured the estrangement of his family. The more he prayed for his mother, the more disturbed she became.

"This shows that the Holy Spirit was working in her heart," Peter said. "So I kept praying . . . harder than ever."

But he returned to the United States without seeing his mother take the step of faith. For several more years he prayed, but letters from home remained cold and indifferent.

"My hope was in Christ," Peter said. "I am happy to say that when I returned home to White Russia again after many years of prayer, my mother met me with open arms, even before I got to the house. She cried out, 'Pyotr, I am receiving Christ as my Savior now!'"

There on the walk to her humble house she broke down and wept for joy. As they approached her house, neighbors started gathering to see what was happening.

His brother, Andrei, a confirmed unbeliever, also came under conviction through prayer. "The more you pray for me the worse I feel, and the more I suffer," he told Peter. So Peter prayed harder. His persistence was rewarded by the salvation of his only remaining brother. God broke that proud, stubborn heart and brought a committed atheist to Himself.

"The effectual, fervent prayer of a righteous man availeth much."

The Slavic Gospel Association was born through prayer and fasting in 1934. Intercession has been the *modus operandi* in the growth and development of the association throughout the world. Every day the office opens with prayer. Once a month the mission has an all-day prayer meeting. Each year staff members and friends of the mission spend twenty-four hours in continuous prayer.

"We always notice how God blesses following these all-day prayer meetings," Peter observed. "Souls are saved, workers encouraged, and funds for the work supplied."

Prayer was Peter's divine weapon for guiding his mission through troubled waters, for raising his three children, for preaching, and for person-to-person soul winning.

He was praying definitely for a fellow Russian in Chicago one time because the young man leaned toward atheism. The Russian laughed at Peter for attending church, but Peter promised: "I will not stop praying for you until God saves your soul."

"Well, you'll be praying for a long time then," the young man replied.

"If you die without God, you'll find out too late in eternity that He exists," Peter warned.

For more than a year Peter faithfully prayed for the man. He also enlisted the prayer support of others. One Friday afternoon a friend of Peter's also agreed to pray for a full two hours on behalf of the unsaved Slavic man.

The following morning Peter went to the Marshall Field store where the atheist worked. As he approached the department the Russian looked up with surprise. "Peter!"

he exclaimed. "I'm so glad you came to see me. Yesterday I had no rest and I thought I would die. I didn't know what to do with myself. I felt miserable."

"Praise the Lord," Peter said. "We were praying for you last night."

"Please don't pray anymore," the friend pleaded. "I'll do whatever you tell me to do."

"You must give your heart to the Lord at once," Peter explained.

The man promised he would the next Sunday. He also promised to be at Moody Memorial Church at 3:00 P.M. for the young men's Bible class.

He was there. When the teacher gave the invitation for salvation, the young fellow walked forward, knelt at the altar and wept, giving his heart to the Lord. He later told Peter of the terrible suffering his heart had endured. With his life straightened out, he married a Christian girl and today enjoys the blessing of a Christian marriage.

"Keep on praying for unsaved friends!" Peter admonishes everyone.

Such incidents were common in the life of Peter Deyneka. He allowed God to lead him to people with hungry hearts, and God kept him busy on fruitful assignments.

Peter's wife is his most faithful and enduring prayer partner. Vera Demidovich learned to pray early in her Christian life, even before she met Peter during his preaching mission to Russia. She began her Christian life under great oppression from an unsaved family and had to lean heavily on the Lord to fortify her against misunderstanding parents, brothers, and sisters. Her lonely spiritual crusade taught her early to pray effectively.

The Deyneka-led prayer meetings in Winona Lake, Indiana, during summer Youth for Christ and other Bible conferences have become legendary. For twenty summers in succession he continued this prayer ministry.

Missionary Hubert Mitchell of Los Angeles felt a kinship

174

Peter's fractured English never was a hindrance in making God's message clear to thousands of young people in Youth for Christ Rallies around the world.

Ted Engstrom and Bob Cook of YFC with Peter Deyneka, whose contribution to the team efforts were super doses of prayer in all-night sessions. These prayers unleashed spiritual power and brought heaven close.

Hundreds of young people were challenged to dedicate their lives to Christ during Peter's frequent visits to Jack Wyrtzen's Word of Life Camp at Schroon Lake.

Peter Deyneka, Jr., often accompanied his father to Bible camps and conferences and caught his father's burden for Slavic people and a vision of what God can do through a dedicated life.

Peter Deyneka, Jr., now executive director of the Slavic Gospel Association, and his father discuss mission expansion.

Peter and Vera Deyneka with their children (who are all active Christians) and their growing grandchildren.

with Peter Deyneka as he participated in the meetings in the old Billy Sunday Tabernacle, and in the hillside services at Winona Lake.

"Peter would literally lay hold of the horns of the altar in nights of prayer," Hubert Mitchell recalled, "when everybody else was falling by the wayside. Peter was constantly laying hold of heaven for evangelism—especially for the Russian nation. I believe those nights of prayer deposited some holy seeds that have many times sprouted and brought forth the harvest not only here but in other countries as well."

During Youth for Christ evangelism conferences in Ireland, Belgium, Venezuela, and Brazil, Peter Deyneka headed the prayer groups.

Robert A. Cook, an early president of Youth for Christ, who later became president of King's College, labeled Peter's ministry "a power quite beyond the natural gifts with which God had endowed him."

Not many days would go by, if Peter was in town, before he would stop in at Bob Cook's office and say, "Well, Brother, let's pray!"

Peter believed that unless prayer became frontal, deliberate, and planned, rather than a luxury or an accessory, the Christian could expect little of a miraculous nature.

Bob Cook grasped that fact early in his leadership. He passed the word throughout Youth for Christ that if young men wanted to remain in top administrative positions within the organization, the price of that leadership would be prayer.

Peter Deyneka's method for long periods of prayer was first a season of prayer . . . then a time of praise . . . then Bible teaching . . . then testimonies from people in whose life God had been working. At the close of the second period of prayer the leader should provide an invitation.

"I've learned that people make their best speeches to God in the early hours of those extended prayer meetings," Bob

Cook observed. "But later on they get around to telling God the real truth about the situation. And sometimes the Holy Spirit of God breaks through to heart and mind and conscience in a way that makes the individual willing to deal with matters concerning which he was quite inflexible two or three hours earlier."

He recalled one young man who prayed a very acceptable prayer along about eleven o'clock. But by one-thirty in the morning, an invitation was given and this same young man said softly with his head bowed, "Will somebody please pray for me? I am not saved."

Some amusing incidents linger in the minds of those who participated in prayer meetings led by Peter Deyneka. One evening he was directing an all-night prayer meeting in the old Westminster Hotel at Winona Lake, Indiana. The group was using what was called the Ball Room in that hotel.

At about 2:00 A.M., Peter Deyneka began to warm up to his usual completely uninhibited fashion. There was no toying with the subject. Prayer requests were boldly pronounced and God was implored for answers.

Peter's energy and fervor probably did raise the volume of his praying a few decibels above normal, making his prayers rise to other floors above the Rainbow Room, the main conference center.

Presently there was a knock on the door. The clerk at the front desk was asking, "Could Mr. Deyneka please lower his voice so guests upstairs could get some sleep?"

One of the men took the message to Peter and tapped him on the shoulder. "You know, Peter," he began, "God isn't deaf."

"No," Peter replied, "and He isn't nervous either!"

He went right on praying without missing a beat.

In another prayer meeting, while praying for a number of people Peter became confused about names and got them all mixed up. He paused for a moment, then said, "Sorry, Lord. Wrong number."

In Charleston, West Virginia, Peter arrived in town for meetings just ahead of the worst blizzard that part of the country had seen in a long time. He and the men gathered with him were literally marooned in their hotel by the storm. Yes, Peter initiated a prayer meeting.

"Lord, why did you do this to me?" he demanded. "You know that I set aside this time to come here for a meeting. You know also that I am busy and that I could hardly spare the time. And here I came to do Your will. Now why do You send a blizzard to stop the meeting? You know my needs. I'm going to trust You to do something special for me."

A handful of people did manage to make it to the meeting that night through the howling storm. One of them gave a large check for the Slavic Gospel Association's missionary outreach. God knew why he had taken Peter Deyneka to Charleston.

One day, while distributing tracts, Peter walked up to a man in Minneapolis who was dressed in overalls and appeared to be despondent.

"Pardon me, may I talk to you?" Peter asked.

The man looked at him in surprise.

"I prayed and asked God to lead me to someone who needed help," Peter went on to explain.

"How did you know I need help?" the man asked. "I have a wife and two children, and here I am out on the street because I was so drunk my wife asked me to leave home. I am brokenhearted. I don't care much for my wife, but I love my two precious children. Now I have no home and there's no hope that things will get better. . . ."

"There is hope in Christ," Peter assured him.

They went to a nearby Gospel Rescue Mission where the lonely man knelt down and prayed, "I need God's help. Pray for me."

His home was two hundred miles from Minneapolis. But Peter received a letter one week later, telling how the man had found a way home, had asked forgiveness of his family,

180

and had been completely restored to them. Prayer had led Peter to the man who needed God.

"It pays to pray that God will lead and guide you to speak to some poor, lost soul about Christ," Peter says with characteristic simplicity. "The Bible says, 'If any of you lack wisdom, let him ask of God, that giveth to all men liberally. . .'

"Because God answers prayer, He has opened doors for us to work and to preach the gospel in more than twenty-two countries around the world, with more than 140 missionaries preaching in twenty languages. Scores and scores of souls are being won for the Lord; thousands hear the gospel who otherwise would never have heard, and much relief clothing and food have been sent to poor Christians in Europe.

"God also heard our prayers regarding our children. My wife and I have had the joy of leading all three of them to the Lord Jesus Christ. I also had the joy of baptizing them. All three have dedicated their lives for the Lord's service and have received training in Christian colleges. Our oldest daughter, Ruth, has been a missionary in Europe and is now in South America, where she and her husband continue to send out the gospel in Russian from Radio Station HCJB, Quito, Ecuador. Our son, Peter Jr., has preached the gospel in Europe, Alaska, the United States, South America, and Canada. Today he is the General Director of the mission. Our youngest daughter, Lydia, has been in the teaching field and is now a homemaker. Together with her husband, she is active in a local church."

Peter Deyneka is a living fulfillment of his motto: "Much prayer, much power." His recipe is simple: "When you go to pray, pour out your heart before God. Claim His promises. Claim the victory. Ask God to cleanse your heart, mind, and even your thoughts. When David prayed he said, 'Try me, and know my thoughts' (Ps. 139:23). He not only asked God to search his heart, but also to search his thoughts.

181

"If we meet God's conditions when we come to pray, He has promised to do His part. Our part is to come to Him, to seek Him, ask of Him, in faith and sincerity with a pure heart, in His name and authority, and He will hear and answer our prayers.

"Do you love the Lord? Then take time to talk to Him. Our prayer of faith will accomplish great things."

15

The Cry from the Steppes

At the Chicago headquarters of Slavic Gospel Association one morning, Peter Deyneka opened an unusual letter from Russia with postmarks indicating the sender lived in the town of Peter's birth:

> On May 13, 1974, in the morning, I heard you preaching here in Russia from Radio Station HCJB. At first I didn't recognize your voice, but later when you gave your name I remembered you. For a long time now I have wanted to hear your voice but never had the opportunity. The broadcast signal that morning was very clear and without any interference. Every word was clear.

Peter wept as he continued to read:

> I still remember your visit to our country forty years ago. From our town you went to the city of Chomsk. There was a big meeting there, during which time many people were baptized. My sister and I attended this meeting and we had to walk fifty kilometers [thirty miles] in order to get there.

It took us an entire day. We weren't tired when we got there because we experienced such great blessing at that meeting which I will never forget. All of this came back to me as I was listening to your voice over the radio, because of the fact that I had met you at that particular baptismal service. From all of my heart I am grateful to God for these broadcasts and for the joy of hearing your voice again. May the Lord bless you and keep you in His work.

As Peter laid the letter on his desk, the years of memories rolled back to 1941 when he stopped at the new missionary radio station HCJB en route home from his first trip to Argentina. His close friend, Clarence Jones, had casually remarked, "Why don't you try preaching over the radio in Russian, Peter? Let's see if any Russians somewhere in the world are listening."

Over thirty years have come and gone. So many Russians in the Soviet Union are tuning in to the gospel broadcasts that Soviet newspapers are discouraging their citizens from listening. Soviet authorities complain publicly about Russian gospel programs from foreign stations pouring over the Soviet Union "like ocean waves." SGA radio workers are careful to use the air waves only for preaching the gospel in obedience to Christ's commands. Politics are not mixed into the broadcasts.

Reports from inside the USSR indicate that millions of Russian citizens have their big shortwave radios set to receive Christian programs.

Peter Deyneka has met many of them during travels throughout Russia. He had only to say his name to have the entire congregation brighten with recognition: "You are the Pyotr Nahumovich who speaks on the radio broadcasts!"

Christian believers all over Russia, like an unseen spiritual bond, have confided to Peter: "We pray and fast on the first Friday every month, asking God to continue to bless and encourage the Church in the West to help us save millions of our people through your broadcasts."

In one church a babushka (elderly grandmother) told Peter with a smile, "The broadcasts drop out of the air like a gift from heaven to us."

Russian Christians are eager to share with Peter stories about how the broadcasts have brought their countrymen to Christ. A man in remote Siberia, for example, had never seen a Bible . . . never attended church . . . never met another Christian. He came to saving faith in Jesus Christ through a message he heard from a radio preacher.

In another town a layman found the courage to preach as a result of listening to the radio broadcasts. After he became a believer he wanted to enroll in a seminary but seminaries are not allowed in Russia. Therefore he listened to the Radio Bible Institute of the Air, produced by the Slavic Gospel Association, and other broadcasts to receive his theological education.

"Whole villages have come to Christ through the broadcasts," Slavic Christians have told Peter. He saw for himself how the broadcasts had become Bible, preacher, and Sunday school for multiplied thousands deprived of these spiritual blessings.

Many letters sent by listeners never get past Soviet censors. But those few thousand each year which are delivered contain interesting stories and comments. The church of Eastern Europe speaks through these excerpts:

USSR

Peace to you, dear brother and all your co-workers. . . . You always ask that we drop you a few lines which would bring you joy and encouragement. Please understand, brother, we would snow you under with letters, but. . . . Having this opportunity to write to you a few lines through Brother F. who is in our midst here in the Soviet Union as a guest from Poland, I would like to briefly give you a few facts. All of us listen to you with joy—not only believers but also unbelievers have a great desire to listen to your programs. At times one walks along the street and hears the voice from Monte Carlo coming from apartments, in spite of the fact that many must listen at a low volume so that no one would discover that they do listen. There are those who have come to repentance listening to the radio in their homes. One backslider, having heard your message, repented and once again follows the Lord. In one village an unbeliever bought himself a radio receiver. His neighbors came to hear just anything and so, as he was turning the dial, they heard wonderful singing. They realized that it was something religious and good and they started to listen. This was on Saturday and you preached. They listened to the message and were deeply under conviction, looking with bewilderment at the radio. They began questioning among themselves, "How is it that he, being so far away, speaks as if he sees us? Listen! He is talking about us!" And they broke down in weeping. That is the way the preaching of the gospel affects the hearers; it is the power of God unto salvation to everyone that believeth. Praise be unto the Lord.

* * *

USSR

Hello, dear friends. Finally I am able to write you. For two years I have been listening to your broadcasts, but have not written because I was serving in the army. I want to pass on some good news: Thanks to the religious broadcasts, I have become a believer and have received Jesus Christ into my heart. The work which you are doing is great and indispensable. I, for one, wish to thank you for broadcasting the Word of God to my homeland. I am twenty-two years old, am single, have secondary education. I am continuing to listen to your broadcasts and would like you to help me get a Bible and gospel literature.

* * *

Czechoslovakia
First of all I want to convey to you heart greetings in the name of our Lord. I am of Polish descent, a Czechoslovakian citizen. I was on a private visit to Russia. I visited many churches and had numerous meetings with brothers and sisters and I am very thankful to my Lord for these opportunities. What I experienced I can never in my life forget. In one White Russian village a great many people were saved only through listening to the gospel through radio. This small church was for a long time isolated, but finally one brother managed to get through into the village. Many churches pray for you. I personally will wait for your answer. We have to be careful.

* * *

So write members of the Slavic brotherhood of believers—a brotherhood which, according to some Russian Christian leaders, numbers as high as six million in the USSR alone. Despite hardships, the church in Russia is not dying. Conversions are not uncommon.

While Christians are still a minority in the USSR, one city in Russia of two thousand people has some seven hundred citizens who are believers. Annoyed at such a high percentage, atheistic officials jeeringly call it "The City of God."

The Russian church, despite its impact on Soviet society, lacks visible organization. It appears almost primitive by the standards of a sophisticated Western church structure. However, the Russian church in all of its adversity and simplicity offers insights to Western Christians, who enjoy a proliferation of church organizations, seminaries, publishing houses, and Bibles.

Peter Deyneka was deeply moved when he preached in the Evangelical Baptist Church in Moscow. Behind him are some of the pastors of the church.

Peter continues to travel worldwide, challenging others to share his burden. As a result, this committee was formed when he and Evon Hedley (standing behind Peter), then Executive Secretary of CBMC International, visited England. Other SGA offices have been opened in Australia, New Zealand, Canada, Bermuda, and Argentina.

At a mission banquet in the Moody Church, Peter Deyneka delivers the annual report to 550 friends and supporters of the SGA.

Peter "Dynamite" today, continuing his dynamic ministry across the United States and around the world . . . challenging Christians to pray . . . with "Much Prayer—Much Power."

The Russian church is a lay church. There are few full-time pastors. Each congregation traditionally has from twenty to forty lay preachers. "This way," explained one church leader, "there are many of us prepared to lead the church. If one is taken, another can step into his place."

It is a lay church, also, because of a lack of Bible schools and seminaries to produce bona fide clergy. With no opportunities for formal Bible training, Russian believers depend heavily on gospel radio broadcasts which are transmitted into the Soviet Union from ten missionary radio stations.

In Russia, Peter Deyneka met hundreds of people who thanked him repeatedly for the radio programs. A lay pastor said apologetically, "I hope you don't mind, brother, that I copy down the sermon outlines from your broadcast so that I can re-preach them to my people. I have no other study materials."

Russian believers feel deeply responsible for missionary outreach. Lay pastors who receive little news of the outside are curious about Christian activity in the West. Freedom there for missionary endeavors amazes them. Other than churches, no religious organizations of any kind exist in the Soviet Union. But the Russian counterpart has its advantages. "You know," said one believer thoughtfully, "here in Russia every Christian is a missionary."

Witnessing in the Soviet Union is not easy. However, many still do. There are no Sunday schools, Christian youth organizations, missionary societies, Bible schools, or evangelical seminaries. There is also a scarcity of Bibles.

But Russian believers pray—and therein lies great spiritual power. Lay pastors pray several times in each service. Others join in total supplication. From all over the sanctuary are heard muffled cries of "Da Gospodyee" (Yes, Lord), in response to the prayers.

When members are given an opportunity to pray aloud there is no hesitation. Prayers from believers with compelling burdens rise in intercession. Often so many wish to participate that the pastor is forced to interrupt and close the prayer session.

There are many things the Russian church cannot do, but believers can pray. One pastor put it this way: "As Christians facing pressures and problems, we can't effectively protest, but we can pray. We can pray as the early persecuted Christian church did in the Acts of the Apostles until the building shakes."

Yet Soviet believers aren't spiritual supermen. They are ordinary people who often become discouraged by their hostile society. But they do not ask to be removed from their country. They plead for the Western church not to forget them. They desire to have evangelistic tools—the broadcasts and Christian books—which they cannot obtain in their own country.

These are the people of Peter Deyneka. For more than half a century he has represented them, speaking out for those who cannot leave, evangelizing many who settled in other lands, placing in their hands the tools for gospel witnessing, and serving as a channel from generous brothers and sisters in free countries wishing to support their beleaguered brethren and sisters.

From one man with a vision, the Slavic Gospel Association has become an international organization with over 140 missionaries in twenty countries touching millions of lives with the gospel of Jesus Christ. Most associates are of Slavic heritage themselves. Some of these missionaries are responsible for the six hundred radio broadcasts beamed into the USSR each month. Some are developing new broadcasts to speak to more young people and to specialized segments of Soviet society. Others deliver the thousands of Bibles and Christian books that cross communist borders each year.

On one autumn day, during his most recent visit to the Soviet Union, Peter Deyneka found himself with a small congregation of believers deep in the heart of Russia. That morning six new converts, robed in white, stood at the front of the church near the baptistry. Each of the six Christians knew the cost of his commitment to follow Christ in baptism. Those who had followed Christ longer had carefully prepared the converts for the momentous step of baptism—a Christian ceremony particularly despised by atheist authorities.

Many of the believers in the congregation held flowers which would later be presented to the person who was prepared to obey Christ by entering the waters of baptism.

The pastor, a humble man in a dark suit and white beard, waited on each candidate as the other Christians sang hymns of praise.

As one of the women was helped from the baptistry, the people gathered around and offered their flowers which she accepted gratefully. When her bouquet was complete she turned to the visitor and extended it. "Brother Deyneka," she said, "you must have these. If it had not been for your radio broadcasts I would not be a Christian today."

Peter took the flowers and bowed. "Thank you, Father," he prayed. "You have not left my people without a witness."

He looked at the flowers. They were nodding in his shaking hand. He knew they were given in thanksgiving for what God had done.

"Da Gospodyee [Yes, Lord]," the people murmured.

The missionary outreach of the Slavic Gospel Association described in this book continues. Further information about the Slavic Gospel Association–the mission founded by Peter Deyneka–can be obtained by writing:

Slavic Gospel Association
P.O. Box 1122
Wheaton, Illinois   60187